Brother Roman

♦

Ω

Credits

Story: Guy Maybriar
Cover Art: Brian Smith
Back Cover Art: Karl Persson
Interior Art: Puis Calzada (Seraphim – Saturn)
Interior Art: Jesse Hanson (Transistor - Winter)
Interior Art: Tom Capung (Blue w/Tanya)
Interior Art: David Hernandez (L.P.T)
Cover Alteration: Guy Maybriar
Interior Alterations: Guy Maybriar
Editor: "Willie_Billie"

Contents

1.	*Introduction*
8.	Seraphim
13.	Helios
19.	Equanimity
53.	Waif
57.	Amour
89.	Saturn
95.	Transistor
101.	Heuchler
108.	Exhale
119.	Omerta
133.	Naraka
153.	Leper
159.	Yin
182.	Paramour
195.	Exome
199.	Rand
208.	Somatic
218.	Oni
225.	Nova
232.	Winter
233.	Soundtrack
234.	Closure
235.	Disclaimer
236.	Blue/Tanya
237.	L.P.T-Review

Pre-Maybriar around 2003-2004, 16-17 years old, with mom. Black & Burgundy was always a favorite combination of mine…next to Blue & White.

◆

Introduction

February 28th, 2018 was the last time I saw her, the last hug & kiss I received from her, and…the last "I love you!" I would hear from her lips without realizing the harsh truth. March 2nd, 2018 was the day I learned, in a harsh environment of sleet & snow, that she was having an affair with another for nearly a year. No goodbyes…phone number disconnected…using her parents as angry conduits to tell me off; shielded through parental cowardice…and lastly…images of pornographic material of the two taunting me.

I stood in front of her building in disbelief, the slush of snow dampening my catatonic body. No tears, anger, or signs of emotion…to go through more than a decade with someone just to become strangers once more after all we've endured. This day marked my one notion: Life is now over. No sense of purpose and no one to alleviate my hunger for human touch…just social isolation to begin a slow death. December 30th, 2018 also marked my toxic departure from my job. This would lead to six months of no income. This cemented my idea that Gaia no longer required me.

However, from March 2018 – March 2019 various events occurred that were abnormal…even for me. This story was FIRST started technically on October 25th, 2009 and it did not finish UNTIL September 9th, 2018. I realized that trying to repair a relationship, where only one person is trying, hindered my efforts to "go pro". Complacency and obesity became my best friends, but not anymore. At the end of May, I poured all my money into my eyes…the twenty-year reign of glasses is finally over. September again…stab through my ear now doc (AKA Sexy/Cute Asian Woman from 'Addicted to Ink'), I want that piercing I've always wanted!

Could there be more, oh most definitely kind reader! October 1st – March 6th, 2019 another story added to the bibliography! It's a secret for now. There is one other secret…March 9th – 16th, 2018…another story done, but it will have to wait for quite some time. If I were to give a hint though, its main actor…is the 'Neutral'…and he has a new partner. Again, not for a long time…

Therefore, as you can see…I want you, reader and my pioneer, to NEVER GIVE UP when all of Hell breaks loose! When relationships break down into dust, when jobs are lost, when there are no final goodbyes just remember: We all die, so become the best version of yourself and do unto others, as you would have them do unto you. Never stop improving. Do not give up and die. All I ask is that you live for me…that is my only favor to ask of you. I will always make time to bend my ear when you are feeling low. I will not discard you. Until my final sigh…

…I will always care.

With all my love,
R.K. aka "Guy Maybriar"

Corrosive bacteria on silver bars join hand in hand with the dead cells of flesh to meet one another. Union made tracks to lead down to your pathetic destination so that they may collect their kickbacks. When they cough, it's more so the universal greeting of the Big 'Rotten' Apple. A body could be dead for days before anyone attempted contact with the supposed cat-napping vagrant. It's a great state to do terrible things in front of walking blind eyes. With emotionless faces and loud headphones, the dead truly did walk amongst us. Tonight was quiet for the metro; reserved seats for warlords.

Good…let's mix the dried coffee floors with a touch of red…

"How far are we?" a disgruntled businessman said to his subordinate.

"We're only a few more stops away sir. Nothing's been reported by the freelancers in the other train cars either," he replied.

"Hoggish fucks best be doing their jobs to the letter. I'm in no mood for fuck-ups this late at night. Tell me again why the hell do I have to use this disgusting public transit instead of the car?"

"Again, I'm sorry sir, but we cannot take any risks with a bomb, sniper, or being surrounded with no way out; using the train, and reserving the other cars for our use, is the best option to protect you and without much delay."

The disgruntled man had an annoyed face on him that caused his subordinate to hesitate on continuing.

"All of those options can also be used for a train, idiot."

"We've taken all precautions by surveying every inch before the train left and only left the first car open to the public to not arouse too much suspicion. It was mostly white-collar to the point of the last one to enter wearing all white on even."

"The next stop is Times Square-42St!" the automated speaker said over the PA.

"So close and still stuck in a goddamn tin, no guarantees yet." the man said lowly to himself.

The man had all cars, except for the very first. Each was filled with mercenaries in civilian outfits to blend in. Electricity shortages caused some of the car lights to flicker on and off repeatedly.

Become mythos one final time...

"Huh?" a guard said in the last car.
"Problem?" another asked.
"I could've sworn I saw a mummy with a suit outside the window glaring at me."
"Goddamn moron, keep saying that and I'll start to think that nutcase is on board. Reports say the two got fed misinformation, and are chasing another train instead. Good thing too..."

The first guard shrugged it off and leaned against the exit door. Sparks emitted heavily from the bottom with the lights flickering off momentarily. Let there be light again...and with me behind the door on the outside. My bandaged face glaring into the car, winking at one of the mercenaries inside.

> A wolf came to pray
> Your tribute to cover alms
> We bring the Rapture…

Like the beginning of battle fatigue, a storm of death erupted; time would stand still for none. The mercenary reached for his gun, but my fist crashed into the window and pulled onto him. It was of little effort, and no pain; a gift from the War Lord for closing my way out in the past. Fluorescent angels slept again, but shots were still fired in the dark. When they reappeared, the man's head was severed.

Hanging by a thread they would say…

"We have a problem, I repeat car...!" the mercenary said, while being interrupted.

A needle-shaped dart thrown from the unseen into his Adam's apple. Now we set the small-big device on the door for a genuine Chinese New Year!

The others were firing off into the door and parts of the ceiling. The body must latch onto the side corner of the train and press heavily into it. If I extended by just an iota, new skid marks would graffiti these walls.

"Times almost up…" I said.

Tick-tock, hit the remote inside the blazer already stupid. It had one request: Fuck me with your thumb, and let me gush with fire!

Lamentations of grown men could be heard echoing these dark pathways.

Detonation: Complete...

The violent eruption presented an opening for me; come inside and take a load off. Most of them were disoriented and on the ground. The presentation of my noir blade was held up into the air to begin the scenario. It has bathed in the trenches, it has dusted many chins, and on good days, we anoint it with pyre!

"Got you!" a hired gun shouted, catching hold of my arm.

"Said the departed..."

A sleeve dart jettisoned into his neck.

"Auribus Teneo Lupum? Not yet."

More cannon fodder tried their luck on me. Another shot fired, and another shot missed. Loose cannons always miss when they're so emotional. The eye gave off the rare obnoxious alarm. The alarm...I'm bleeding!?

"Not my face...NOT MY FUCKING FACE!" I screamed.

SERAPHIM

The trench was plunged deep into his temple. His eyes screamed with violence, and behold there was red fluid from all openings of the skull.

A shame I could not bring my "little helpers" for this one time, but in case this fails they need to safeguard my Stoic and Huntress...I miss my little blue dragons and yellow carnivores. The Huntress was not pleased with me dismissing her help.

The final marksman held up the blasted door and marched forward with the makeshift shield. The knife won't help; maybe the arm of science or the secret cannon? His silhouette grew closer; obscenities excreted as if censorship had been purged.

Patience was the key and our reactions would meet shortly. His heavy breathing grew louder; the joust commenced. The opposite car door opened, but our acts already met each other.

"What the hell's going on in here!?" a mercenary shouted.

"Get down!" the shielded mercenary screamed at the top of his lungs.

"Accipe hoc!" I shouted unleashing another dart.

No time to see it connect, I had to rush the shielded shooter. A flurry of punches commenced through the broken window. A closed coffin will be in order for your face good looking...

"You're going to need a new Maxilla big guy." I said lifting my head up.

My dart hadn't stayed true to the course it would seem. Only a trail of blood was left behind with no corpse to ease my mind.

"How is car five?" a voice said from under my collar.
"Cleared, I am now proceeding to the fourth. Cover has been revealed, proceed cautiously."

So much blood was on me and my suit. Etiquette demanded a presentable look before proceeding to the next car, but time is of the essence.

"What the fuck is going on in there!?" the businessman said to his subordinate, "Go check it out now! I knew this was a bad idea; it has to be those two assholes…if only I had finished Eddy back in the bunker…"

The underling drew out his gun and made his way towards me.

"Only a couple of more minutes, wait minutes, why's the goddamn train slowing down!?"

No "I" in team, another actor rises to the occasion of downfalls.

A man in car one rose up from his seat to walk casually over to the second car's door. A presentation of all white with blue, he was an ivory man with a suitcase in hand. A hired gun on the other side of the door prompted him that the car was closed off to everyone. The man in white nodded and grinned.

"With science and faith, all shall rise."

Taking a step back, he threw his briefcase on the floor. The lights had once again blacked out temporarily. When they reappeared, a drone was before them; hovering with ill intent.

"What in the fuck?" the hired gun said.

Beams of light crashed into the car, for blitzkrieg performed its horrific opulence. A bullet made contact with a gunman in the target's car. The top half of his skull vanished, and with no life did his body fall onto the businessman's lap. The corpse had its tongue flapping around with some teeth dropping out of the gum line.

The tunnels are alive with the bellowing of screams.

"This can't be happening. It just can't!" the businessman screamed.
"Car two and someone from three have been taken care of. How's your four?" the man in white spoke into the microphone.
"Drunker than Dionysus!"
"Idiot…our stop is approximately less than 30 seconds; if you really want the target you better get a move on!"

Dropping a torn arm, I started to make haste. I'll get the bastard that severed mine! However, a man with a gun was pointing it at me.

Is today the day I see you mother?

"Pull it...end it now...become the hero...PULL IT BOY!"

He was too frozen to even move. His eyes were fixated onto my exposed left eye. Cybernetics have become highly sought after, now that they're mostly perfected; if you had the money. Walking nonchalantly to him, he started to shake the gun even more. The eye saw a very interesting probability on my survival rate...should he jerk the trigger, the rate of succession would be 97%.

"Next time shoot. Never aim a gun at someone unless you intend to use it. Otherwise...hesitation will kill you. Get out of this business before you ruin this beautiful suit of yours."

He dropped the gun and huddled against the doors; uncle once told me of this kind of cowardice when he was growing up...we get older, but time keeps recycling the old ways with each new generation.

"What the hell is this!?" I yelled as I tiptoed around corpses.

The target was also amongst them...

HELIOS

"You took your fine time, and I had to fulfill the contract before the doors opened. Sorry little man." the man in white said holstering his gun.

Annoyed, I sheathed my knife back inside my suit. We both stood next to each other in front of the double doors in silence. Silence in New York is by far the eeriest of moments.

"This stop is Times Square-42St!" the automated speaker said over the PA.

We stretched our backs in unison, once we exited: Job Complete.

"Freeze!" a brigade of cops said pointing guns at us.

"I thought you said you paid off the conductor?" I asked.
"I did, but I guess he tried to pull a fast one thinking the police would take us down in a hail of gunfire."
"You two should be dead right now, but I have orders from the Chief to hold fire until I receive it. Failure to show it to me will result in the gunfire becoming a dream come true for this country," a cop said approaching us.
"Captain DelGuidice! What a wonderful surprise as always good sir!" my partner replied.
"Cut the bullshit, I want it now as proof of this massacre."
"My, my, you shouldn't overwork yourself. After all, it was us who took care of a very big weapons dealer who's

wanted in several countries for a large list of naughty things."

I stood quietly staring at the floor with a tired look. A good portion of my stamina was used and I was too languid to deal with the police. The man in white slowly reached into his once impeccable blazer for what the captain had asked for. Some of the cops had uneasy looks on them, and some cocked the hammers on their guns. I can picture the newspaper articles now…

"Easy boys, if I had wanted to make a bloodbath with you we wouldn't have exited so casually, now would we?"

He laughed while taking out the item in question, and handed it to the captain. Never has the Captain read paperwork this quickly in this life, but there are a plethora of reasons as to why.

"It says that any sort of public damage that's been committed must be paid for immediately or the contract is void even if successful."
"But of course, and I've wired the funds straight to the city. I've contributed quite enough for possibly a whole new circuit of trains. Penn-Station could use a bit more help since I hate being tardy while traveling during the holidays. Now that you have your writ, my brother and I will take our leave. I've had one of my drones whip up the exact analytics sent to you, the Chief, and other members in City Hall," my brother said making his exit.

One cop stepped in his way to block his path. Now he's done it…

"You know we have a whole squad here that can rid you and your bandaged freak of a brother. What's stopping us from taking you both out and letting both New York and this country sleep a little easier?" he said with a gun in hand.

"Rodriguez you're out of line, step back!" The Captain ordered.

"Stopping you? Why…nothing of course. You can pull it now…end our lives…and go home tonight a hero." He replied, "…But, I always make sure to know who's accompanying 'who' before meeting the individual. So, seeing I'm to meet the Captain afterwards I'd figure…hey, who else am I meeting that's a part of his division? Who's tagging along in the background while my brother and I risk our necks because local P.D. can't get the job done? Who's itchy for us, and wants to ride the Captains coattails in hopes of a situation…just like this?"

Tension is building, and the eye is painting too many for us to handle; future predicaments point to fear…one piece of lead to the head to make it all go away…years of trying to troubleshoot my way to peace is always a sigh away…

"So, I've read everyone's files and you have some kids don't you, Rodriguez? It would be a shame though if your children didn't make it to Christmas. Tragic irony; I think not, seeing as it leads to a raw act of poetic justice with an insurance plan. And even though our bodies are slain in the cold pools of blood, so would your children's. We all know one of them is a hemophiliac. Imagine just...one...cut. And what can you do to us!? Though dead we are nothing more than two sides of Duncan laughing in death at Macbeth who cannot damage us anymore than he already has. Make a move or be a man...your choice piggy."

Mephistopeles couldn't make those words sound anymore vile if he were present. The cop stepped to the side and the rest as well lowered their weapons.

"I'll fucking get you...both of you! I'll especially get you Eddy, you goddamn demon!"

"Rodriguez that's enough!" the Captain shouted.

"Is he a human or a demon!? Nobody knows, Collin de Plancy would too be bewildered as to how to classify me." I said in a sarcastic tone.

"Here's a gift from both me and my brother to you for a job well done Captain," brother said tossing him a gift-wrapped box.

"What is this?" the Captain asked.

"A promise I made a long time ago. Have a Merry Christmas, and remember the next time we do this sort of thing, don't interrupt us prematurely. You should be dealing with that conductor as technically he's stolen from us. The writ states that anyone who's cooperated with us and goes against the contract must be incarcerated to the fullest extent of the law without say."

I followed behind him heading to the street level. Winters embrace welcomed us once again 'peace' would have to be met another time I suppose.

"Captain over there!" an officer shouted.

He pointed to the underling who was sitting up against a beam; evidence with the mask of panic.

"Take him in."

A light flurry of snow softly blew down, another long night of the usual; kill or be killed for a foreign desire. This was to be the final though. This was to lead to retirement after six years. Maybe I'll part ways with this country for good…don't think the 'huntress' would like that though; she would definitely stalk until I've submitted.
But…sometimes it feels better to just give up and surrender for the right reasons.

Mom, I miss you.

"I really can't enjoy the snow with all these lights." My brother said looking around.
"…"
"Speak your mind, Eddy. I hate it when you close yourself to socialization."
"Tired and really hungry as well. Plus I hate being in Manhattan, you know that."
"I know, but we need to clear the shit we've done to walk in the streets freely again. Come on let's take a walk

EQUANIMITY

over to 46th. I know a great hotel nearby that has some great food in the mezzanine and their bar is of relaxation. We can discuss further matters there, and don't worry about your appearance when we get inside."

"I doubt they can serve us food and drink at this hour, Anthony."

"Nonsense we're 'celebrities' and the news on this will be everywhere for all to see. Let me check the time anyway." he said pulling out his pocket watch.

"When did you acquire a Super complication?"

"The buyer got into a little bind with Laurent and long story short gave me the watch in exchange for their life. How could I resist," he replied cheerfully.

"Well, aren't you lucky. Speaking of luck, I'm thinking about jumping ship finally; bounty hunting is mundane, and I want to retire into my house on the coast."

"…Your bosses aren't as considerate as mine is. We still need to discuss more about them."

We ventured forth to the hotel to plan more about our future works. Anthony was always the smart one, but something didn't quite match in this situation. Of course nothing is without recompense, and two kids from Nereid Ave. would definitely have more problems than solutions. One goes to aristocrats, and the other belongs to a complicated clandestine association. One has a painting aging in the attic, and the other…has a long story of regrets.

"Coming to you live in New York, its channel 54's number one news team! With your hosts Sue Smalls, Ernie Rollins, and Alex Dario," a television narrator spoke aloud.

"Good morning New York, I'm Sue Smalls and here's the news. Earlier this morning a bloodbath occurred on the 2 train over on 42St. Arms dealer Julio Valentine was amongst the bodies that were found in one of the train cars, along with more than several bodyguards that were found killed in a brutal fashion. No eye witnesses have been reported as of yet and N.Y.P.D has refused to give out any information. One arrest has been made so far. Reports say that the man arrested was one of Valentine's personal bodyguards and is the only survivor that was found at the scene. Many citizens believe it was caused by the Roman Brothers, as they were spotted in a nearby area. The President is currently preparing to make a speech concerning them later today. We'll keep you updated as the day progresses. Now, a short word from our sponsor."

"Does the word remake, or repetitive, make you cringe!?" an ecstatic man said on the television.

Bullets crashed into the television, and sparks of electricity crackled through the debris of crucified circuitry. A pale man in an ill-fitted suit held out a smoking gun. His eyes bulged through his sunken in sockets. A seamless scowl painted across his toad-like face. With a rolled-up hundred dollar bill, he proceeded to do a sprint of lines on his rosewood table. The wrinkles from his apparel looked better than his nostrils.

"Goddamn brothers. I knew that schmuck would wind up dead using the subway. One of you pricks go find me a new dealer. I need a new supplier who can offer both product and protection. Tell them money isn't an object. I got bored rich kids snorting my shit day in and out hungry for my delicacies."

His guards exited in a haste. Never make a kingpin wait, especially those with addled minds. Their thought process is to rape the land for its resources; pillaging any man's land, and take the women prisoner for their own organic highs of dopamine to render them in a lackadaisical mind field.

The Governors Ball hides many of these sick fiends that parade themselves as "vegan", but that's the trap to ensnare the weak-minded...

"They could've been on my side, but no 'drugs are bad and so is supplying it'. A pair of pussy is knitted neatly together. They got no problem killing, but god forbid substances touched their lives they'd have a shit fit. Fuck it. My contracts' just came in and before they get close to me I'll be out of this shithole recession country. Good thing Ms. 'BZ' vouched for me to the other three, it'd be fucking hell getting this new product moved without them." He mumbled with a constant snort.

The Big Apple is littered with many hotels that act as their own countries. Good thing Anthony knows where the proper asylums are; uninformed police would create a scene before the big news about us was leaked officially.

The proprietor compensated our rooms for a previous favor. Apparently, one of Valentine's associates was trying to strong-arm him into selling the establishment. From the description he gave us I think he's being scrapped off the platform.

If people only knew how much we make them sleep easier…

A phone call from Anthony awakened me, telling me to meet him in the Mezzanine Restaurant. Stumbling to the bathroom was never a good start when reapplying the bandages to my face. Unearthly migraines began to set in. The incident will never cease knocking on my cranium; as that couldn't get any more literal. It's best to keep my eyes halfway closed while cleaning my face. Even while living in such a 'progressive' state, my face has always been uninvited well before I took up the blade; especially now since we'll be able to walk the streets freely again.

God bless America for our constant greed!

A gentle knock ruminated through the silent suite. The entertainment suite; how baronial for my tastes, the pugnacious Spaniard thought to himself. A bell boy was present.

"Sorry to bother you sir, but this was to be delivered to you."

He handed me a wrapped suit coat, and a box, with shaking hands. His refusal to look at me directly already annoyed me. A tip for the hop should suffice for the annoyance to pester off. Awe presented itself when opening the gifts. A single-breasted overcoat and the box contained an assortment of highly sought after cigars.

The Mezzanine was calling, but the common air of odious stares was very much present. If I wasn't the man I am now, these upscale animals would snort profusely with stink glares. Why can't you just enjoy your $30 of 8oz of H2O?

Shady rubbernecks…

Slowly making my entrance, the proprietor was on standby for yours truly. With an approach of gratitude, he shook my hand telling me how grateful he was for ridding the associate. His initiative led me over to one of the tables where Anthony was.

"How are you feeling this morning sir?" the proprietor asked.
"I'm feeling quite relaxed now thank you. The music selection is choice."

They were playing Stings "Fragile".

"Bout time you woke up," Anthony said.
"The lark said to the night owl."

A snicker sounded off.

"Yes, well I'm ready to order now. I'll have my usual Mediterranean cuisine with sparkling water and my brother will have the chicken marcel blanc, with steamed vegetables, mashed potatoes, sweet of course, and also with sparkling water." Anthony said to the waiter.

What is the fascination behind carbonated water?

"…Am I not allowed to make my own decisions?" I asked.

"You can, but my drone picked up several deficiencies in your body. I can't help but notice that your healers are over-exerting themselves to the point where they need to recharge more so often. You promised me you would take better care of yourself since your latest surgery…isn't Cosme's people doing well by your new wing?"

"They are, but she is more interested in replicating another data associate after my failure from the bunker incident. V should've never saved me…" I replied.

A disconnected appendage, in place of wires, was an alien concept to me. Even a faux epidermis layer to hide away the construct, could not ease my constant anxiety. How we take for granted the things we once had, and now I must take longer warm showers to imagine the gentle touch of lost sensations.

Pathetic excuse of male…

"I'm going to ignore that considering T and the 'Stoic' are always by your side. Also, another 'data' associate? One of those costs more than all the blue collars she and her online affiliates had replaced almost a decade ago. I've never read about so many suicides in my life!"

"We're making use of those in our private shelters, and ex-military are protecting our most vital cache. We're better employers than this useless government."

"True...changing topics: I see you're enjoying your gifts."

"Why wouldn't I?"

"Right, well after this I have to take my leave and report back to the 'tower'. Some unfortunate news came across my desk stating that Valentine was another pawn to something bigger. I know this is not what you want to hear...considering what he did to you last year, but at least we put him down for good after evading us for this many years. My advice to you is to take some time off until I can gather more data on the situation. You have plenty of money to retire several lifetimes, why not invest it? All you need to do is put the money in the machine and relax."

I was quiet and I looked around the restaurant. It was not rare to see how some of the people turned their heads and eyes as quickly as I made contact.

"You and I both know it's too late to go legit. Look at me. I wasn't meant to be a husband, a lover, or bland enough to be looked at without people turning their heads. I was never..." I said being interrupted.

"That's enough Eddy. There are plenty unfortunates in this world who have it far worse than you. Self-care should be your main priority. Let it come naturally at this point: health equals wealth. Best not to let your problems overwhelm you, otherwise they're living in your head rent-free."

I kept quiet for several minutes, which seemed like hours, while he continued to counsel me. For once the waiter came to save the day.

"Our food is here; let's enjoy our time together before we split again."

Kill the mute air.

"Merry Christmas Anthony."
"And a happy Festival of Lights to you Eddy. Before you go I'm going to have to steal one of those cigars from you."
"You're not getting the Opulence flavor, just to warn you."
"You just love that cocoa and cinnamon don't you? Pass the Decadence then."
"The lady killer requests a cognac eh?"
"Speaking of, have you heard from the beauty of Kentucky?"
"The 'Blood Diamond' of Louisville...she's still without a trace. It's probably for the best. I stopped asking T since she goes on a tirade of not knowing anything. Those two never did get along for some reason."
"I still think she knows the answer and refuses to tell you considering she found out the history of you two. You did more than apprentice 'under' her after all. Moreover, I heard a rumor, she fled to Belarus, I remember my contract

there…sticky business. If you truly lost interest in T, why not take a trip and get yourself hitched to Ms. Kentucky?" he said laughing.

"Euphrosyne of Polotsk didn't give us her blessing, so eat!"

A simple tap of glasses silenced the past.

Whatever became of that muse? Like the lost ashes of my cigar, a ghost. Women have a complex way of going underneath the bandages to see the imperfection. Always questions, less answers, nothing but riddles. When I think a new dressing to the face is being clean, it's really another way of wrapping me in my own sins.

We went our separate ways once more. I decided to call my group to see if there were any updates on Valentine's case. As I was pulling out my cell phone, an old lady approached me and decided to spit on my face. Onlookers decided to watch the situation with some pulling out their phones to record.

"You're pure evil!" she roared.

Annoyed, I had the eye scan her I.D. from her purse. She noticed the bright shine examining the item and held it tighter than a miser.

"Now I know where you live."
"Help police!"
"Hey you!" a nearby cop shouted in our direction.
"He's threatening me!"

"We don't have a problem, do we sir?" I said grinning at the officer.

"...Ma'am, I don't see a problem here please move along."

"I noticed you have a bad heart; it won't be long now before the clock stops on its own," I said slanting my body over her.

Her eyes were seething profanities at me, but a gentle cold sweat was also being produced. I have no time for this nonsense. The quick prompt of exiting was done without a second thought.

"Why didn't you do anything? I'm reporting you!" the old woman yelled at the cop.

"Lady, didn't you hear the news about the Roman brothers today?"

More people stared at me with some making a wide berth to let me by. They're making my presence too obvious. It's best to resume my phone call...

"Yes, I want everyone present for this meeting. I'll be there in an hour and a half. The news is already posted?" I asked my associate.

I looked up to see the nearest big screen with the title "Roman brother pardoned" being reported. It was plastered everywhere from small screens to scrolling texts. The eye alerted me of multiple hostiles in the area; all were pedestrians with some hiding weapons on their person.

With a thousand eyes staring at me, and none with good intentions, I knew I overstayed my visit to the big city. Entering the nearest automated cab only one thought came to mind.

No one is innocent in New York…

No better hiding spot than dead land in the boroughs; therein a major facility was located. Despite this, caution must always be taken into consideration when descending to the basement. There was always a jumper biding time to grab you from behind with a broken beer bottle. Police never responded to this location…tax dollars working hardest at the local watering hole.

The eye synched with the hidden doorway.

"Please place I.D. to scanner," an automated voice said. "Security…security…security…"

I revealed my reconstructed eye to have it scanned at closer proximity. With the eye recognized, the door opened to reveal several members of the group standing by.

"What you got for me?" I asked.

"Valentine's connections got him a viable buyer: "The Meprodine". If I remember right he offered you, and your brother, to work for him when you guys were just starting out several years ago," an underling stated.

"J.J.'s resurfaced? 'Bout time he has. He needs to be snuffed off quicker than his coke lines. What's confusing is the fact that Valentine is an independent arms dealer that has antagonized the association for years. He knew we had a priority contract on him for years. So why risk coming back? Plus, the bosses didn't mention anything prior. If the POTUS didn't contract my brother and me, he would've slipped through no problem…none of this makes sense."

"There's more to be said in the meeting room." She replied.

Entering the conference room, the eye picked up the same alerts like back in Times-Square. The tension was brimming, and these were killers in their own departments. Friendly associates stared at me with neutral malice…good thing the suit is also stab-proof for the back.

"Before we begin, is there anyone who isn't here that I am possibly overlooking?" I asked. "Only Caesar."An underling replied.

"Despite him being stabbed several times recently, the injuries themselves were luckily minor. As I recall you used an upgraded smart polymer with a temporary healer attached. That doesn't give him an excuse of not being present. Especially due to the fact he has you people who were handpicked by Noelia herself."

"While this is true he decided to get up in the middle of the night to use the bathroom without any support. With no support, his wounds ruptured and he immediately began bleeding all over the floor. We were able to patch him up again in O/R before further damage was caused. He's currently resting in his room now with a remote monitor keeping us updated. We have him being well acquainted to intravenous treatment."

"...I sometimes wonder why the bosses won't allow me to run my own nest; politics never appealed to me. Caesar best remember that medical funds dry up quicker than our research money. Topic change: Valentine contract. Last night, Tony and I finally dealt the killing blow to his latest operation, with Valentine also. Captain DelGuidice has received the writ issued to us by none other than the POTUS."

Murmur of discontent immediately erupted, and for a good reason. With both the writ and the pardon coming from the President, everyone would choose either my union...or the bosses' side. But I've known for a while they haven't been thrilled with me as of late. Keeping Valentine's presence a secret from me was a taboo after what he did to me.

Every revolution comes with an execution...
...And every war has its turncoats.

Causality will reveal the exhibition of disloyalty soon enough.

"Also, because of this pardon...we are retiring from the contractor's game and have put ourselves as bounty hunters instead." I continued.

More jaws dropping...

"...So...with that said, let us continue our discussion on what we've learned from the V-Case." I said.

My underling brought up an image of the dead bastard's face and file for all to see.

"Julio Valentine was an arms dealer wanted for aggravated assault, larceny-theft, counterfeiting, rape, vandalism, and of course weapons law violations. Last night he was going to meet..." my underling continued.

"He's in for a shit storm now." one member whispered to another.

"I heard a big contract is been put on his head," the second whispered.

"Like that's any news to me? Since when does he not have one put on him?"

"One of my guys in Chelsea heard one of the big wigs from another group got a non-member to fulfill the contract, supposedly from overseas. Oulu…"

"Alright, that's good enough for today. Let's all resume our duties. I'll be in the O/R if anyone needs me." I said to the group.

While we made our way to exit the room, I heard someone behind me clearing their throat; a small bead of sweat forming under the bandages.

"Everyone else is dismissed besides the grandiose ghoul," a voice said.

I turned to notice that the three monitors behind the podium lit up with my superiors on screen. Some of the members were talking amongst themselves while my underling closed the doors behind. My right rotator cuff injury decided to act up…

"Great choice of words as always…sir," I said to my second boss.

"I'd keep that smart mouth of yours shut Eddy," my first said.

"You mind telling us what the fuck's going on Edward!?" the second shouted.

"My brother and I have called it quits on blood money. We're finalizing our 'W2s' to the President, and would like to return to the public again."

"That is not the answer we expected to hear Eddy," my third responded.

"Return to the public…with that mug? And even if you didn't have a mummified face what would you do with your so-called 'freedom'? Who would even try to associate with the likes of you or your brother? What happened to you huh? We took you in because the GOP party didn't want anything to do with you. You showed us so much promise too. I remember a time reading some of the best stories regarding you: 'The Faceless Animosity', 'Decapitated like Cattle', 'The Teutonic Blood-Saw', and my favorite 'The Lamb of Macabre'. In today's paper, it reads 'The Midnight Corpse Train' to which I was happy to see. However, my associates have handed me another paper that reads 'The Good, the Bad, and the Forgiven'. Working for the fucking President!? How dare you enact these decisions on your own you troglodyte! When did your balls become big enough to outgrow your trousers!?" my second screamed.

"This is not acceptable, thus you will deny the pardon and resume your bi-weekly contracts," my first said.

"This is not up for any type of discussion and negotiation is out of the question," my third said backing the others.

"You have 72 hours to give us your answer. I am disregarding this conversation because I expect to see your old self-returned. With us...or against us," my second said.

The monitors turned off simultaneously afterward. Removing their ears off the doors, the two gossiping members grinned at each other and left the base. I inhaled deeply and made my exit to resume my daily surgery. Several members began to prep the machinery, and I removed several articles of clothing before lying on the table.

"How bad was it?" my underling asked.

"Don't worry about it, just the usual gruff. Don't let T know about this...she gets too aggressive in situations like this. I'm ready now."

One of the members placed a mask over my nose and released anesthesia into it. Normally this was my favorite part: sleeping. The health benefits it presented were always a gift. But, something was amiss. My vision had begun a thrill of deception. An opaque world with only a small circle of light was surrounding me.

Why am I standing? Where were the faint whispers of the sandman? Another light beamed onto another figure across from where I stood. I studied the familiar clothing with their back to me. Trying to communicate with them proved impossible. My vocals were muted and neither a whisper nor a scream could be heard. The figure did not respond to anything, just standing with their body moving slightly side to side. Movement…motions…how can I forget to mimic the basics? Right before left as the youth said. Nil? Paralyzed!? The arms were still able to move, but the idea set a weird cog in motion.

A sharp pain grew in them. Movement under the clothing…no…under the skin! Blood seeped from my wrists. God, you cunt, what infernal pain are you bestowing on me…and without sound to be heard, to be helped! Blistering sounds of the underground incited a cacophony of white noise within the canals. Violent holes from my skin and they emerged before me. Ophiophagus Hannah twins, why have you forsaken my temple? They went into their defensive posturing and extended their hoods simultaneously.

Never shall I yield to a pair of squamata horrors!

Shutting my eyes tightly, the unnerving tinnitus drifted away. I felt a coiled formation around the forearms. A sensational light show occurred when I peeked out. They had transformed into sleeve darts. Invictus maneo; now let us observe my newest gifts.

Two distinctions between them: Purple equipped to the left wrist and red equipped to the right. If I couldn't mobilize the legs, maybe my arms would act as a messenger. The red became engulfed in fire and the heat was burning my sleeves! Reacting on instinct, I ejected it towards the ground by the figure. The light, from the unknown entity, instantly shut off. I panicked a little as the black world started getting colder. My breath started to show itself through the brisk air. The throat started to become tighter and I started to gag. Placing my fingers on my neck, the feeling of my veins protruded intensely.

The sounds of my own blood could be heard in my head…this is starting to feel like the Asylum contract all over again! Is that psychopathic shepherd's poison still flowing in me?

Incoherent voices roamed the vapors around me. The mechanized eye became inoperative now. I prayed it would turn on again, even if to show the Indian-head test pattern. Will this stop!?

Stay calm…this is what every enemy wants: panic.

My left arm became numb and acted on its own. Struggling to keep it in place the sheer force was just too much. It commanded the wrist to activate the second dart. The explosion happened in mid-flight like some firecracker and released several falling lights. Some of the falling stars fell behind me, and in a short moment revealed the figure behind me now. Panic has resumed. The figure placed their head on my shoulder and whispered into my ear.

"You have a beautiful apple."

Her voice was beautiful and soft, but no hints of comfort. Confusion held me until she started caressing my neck.

"Let it be mine."

The light around us thinned to an inch. To be blinded only to an inch of life was pure trepidation. She wrapped her arm around my waist and held tightly. My arms began to stiffen as well as my neck. I was now limited to moving my mouth and eye. I noticed a gleam of light being rendered sideways.

Peripheral vision managed to take a glimpse at it. It rendered again, but this was when I noticed it wasn't light. It was the reflection off the side of a serrated blade. I tried screaming for help, but silence was the only thing conjured. The stainless steel of death was now pointed directly at my Adam's apple. The cold air and protruding veins helped me feel every little detail. Slowly pushing it into my neck, violent motions from my eye rattled about. I was sure to see the little grey cells dying through POV with how far back my eye was.

Is she here to collect my dues!?

With the blood pouring out of the wound soundly, the white noise resumed once more; the feeling of being cast away was now tangible. The surgeon's hands slowly pulled out the knife, making sure each nerve could feel every inch from the sadistic procedure. Eventually, it was held up to my face sideways once more, but it revealed her eyes to me. All I saw was a gorgeous set of emerald eyes.

Sweet tender beauty, how your repose in death is such a turn on...I'm more fucked in the head than I thought.

The Shepherd's poison hasn't fully detoxed from me, I'm sure of it now…

The void was back, and the feeling of pain faded away. However, I heard faint echoes; incomplete sentences. "Hold...Down...Critical!" were the only words I could comprehend. They began to speak more coherently and the opaque words were sounding more polished now.

"I said hold him down! Inject him with the relaxant!" a voice shouted.

Moments afterwards, my eyes began to open groggily and I noticed the crew looking over me.
"I want you to run a few more tests on him," a member stated to the rest of the group.
"Sir if you can hear me follow the light as best as you can," he said to me.

He was opening my eyes and shining a light on them. Helios, your machinations are too bright for these weary oculars, even the false one wasn't responding properly…some static.

"Alright mark him down as PERRL. Sir, you just suffered from a case of hyperreflexia. We injected you with a dose of diazepam so you should feel more relaxed now. Your reconstruction needed to be put at a halt though. We should continue this tomorrow when your body gets some R&R."

I tried to reply but was unable to; I was mute. Panic started to set in and my first response was to reach for my neck. No unnecessary lacerations thankfully…

"Yes…you're also suffering from acute laryngitis from your screaming while you were under. Nothing serious of course, your voice should return within a few hours. I'm sure your healers have started working on the issue," he continued.

Irritated, bewildered, but relieved. Some of the members helped me rise, and to wipe some of the sweat from my body. My underling passed me my clothes and asked how I was feeling. Pulling my phone out and typing the words "Girl Dream" to show him, his confused look showed he was unable to interpret it, but left it alone. Gathering the last of my belongings, I sent him one more text.

No messages for today...

Free again, and it nearly took a decade! Most criminals could only dream of this. The thought alone brought a prodigious feeling in me. At first, I was a bit skeptical thinking this may have been obsolete in my case, compared to Anthony's. But the rush to go out now publicly in full view, regardless for my own safety, revived a past powerhouse in me; ominous, entwined with a hint of adrenaline.

Maybe it was because some idiot would shoot me in the head from a distant window; down and out for the count, ignoring all the warnings from the eye. Being mute at the moment would allow no one to hear my last wail to the sky, but the thud of my body to tremble and die. A certain earworm wriggled into my canals from nearby. Best to hum it out while venturing forth so as to grow bored of it.

In a way, I wished I had lived in the certain 'negative' customs of Japan where the denizens would pass you by if you looked like trouble. In the States, however, trouble equals pointed fingers and stared faces. Most times it would escalate depending on how serious the matter, and by the looks of certain people that I passed I was a goddamn beacon for a firefight to happen. Science, as well as the law, was on my side this time 'round.

Turning into a few areas for sightseeing, I noticed a small crowd of people ahead in a circle. It'd be best to avoid trouble by crossing the street and ignoring them.

No looks...no trouble...I hate jellyfish...

"Please stop!" a girl's voice shouted.
"Come on B you know you want to go out with me," a male said.

Looking to the adjacent street, I noticed a girl was in the center of four males. I had the false eye scoop in to see the problem: tears were running down her cheeks. Some ancestral anger always burned bright at the sight of mournful women.

Let's see how this plays out...

"I...I just want to go home Eric! Please let me through!" she whimpered to him.

The male approached her and lifted her head, against her will.

"Why are you crying? My knife doesn't scare you, does it? It's to protect you after all not harm you. Come on cutie."

She closed her eyes and shook her head. He grew furious and lunged at her.

"No!" she screamed falling to the ground.

She cringed and closed her eyes tightly. Silence in the air, and even birds did not dare to peep. Curiosity told her to open the eyes to reveal why nothing came to pass. Only a gasp let loose from her throat at the sight before her now.

With one hand gripping the back of his neck, the other was placed against the back of his head. I was twitching to flick a dart through him, but civility must be set apart from the animals…and I am no longer a denizen to that world anymore.

Intimidation could still be used though…

Wrenching his body to the others, I pulled some of my bandages down to reveal the false eye. They immediately knew who was before them now. Moreover, they were able to see the fiery glow from it. They ran for dear life without so much as helping their friend I still had in my custody. This world is filled with too many chicken-hearts. Flipping him on his back, I crouched over him, neutrality scrawled over my face. His reaction was no different from the others.

"Please Mr. Roman! Don't kill me! I'll do anything!!" he screamed.

I smacked him and held a finger to my mouth to signal silence from him. My voice had returned, but I had a better idea. Signaling the female to me, I spoke simple words to her. She stood up and looked at his blubbering face. It took her a second to say them, but she said them fiercely once she realized he and his softies would have their way with her.

"Piss yourself…" she said to him.

I waited a few moments, but nothing…he needed an incentive. Drawing forth my knife, I rubbed it across his face with the point going lower and lower until it stopped at the crotch. The initiation took place with him grunting a bit, and warm fluid spilling from his baggy pants to the cold sidewalk. With the steam rising, I myself rose up from the disgust to hold a tissue against my nose.

"Drink…more…water," I said coughing.

He fled before I could finish. It was a goddamn mistake to think I could just go for a fucking 'casual' walk like some basic plebian. When it all comes down to it, I am still a deformed contractor…I just have nothing better to do now besides figuring out how to answer the bosses. So many contracts, not enough R&R…best to head home and see how base is taking the news. I have been ignoring T's messages. Eventually, she will send out everyone to bring me back by force if need be. When did she become so clingy?

It was definitely after the disappearance of Leila no doubt...

"Wait!" the girl's voice shouted.

My back was already facing her, but I decided to stand firm to hear what she had to say.

"You're…the real Edward Roman, aren't you? The people who pretend to be you can't fake your eye."

I did not respond back besides placing one foot in front of the other. Do not get mixed up with her old boy, leave without a care.

My footsteps sounded different; Echo are you confusing me for Narcissus? The eye showed that the girl was following me. I do not need this problem, bad enough I have to deal with the huntress at home base.

"Um...I was wondering if I could maybe walk with you for a bit. Those people will definitely be after me if you leave. I'm…also kind of a fan of your work," she said.

Christ almighty, mother…I thought Tony and I killed off all of the Shepherd's flock! I looked at her from top to bottom: petite, curvy, long black hair, and…well I am not getting into this one…

"Just take a car back; I'll even pay the fare."
"…I'd rather not go home."
"Kid I don't believe in goddamn groupies…I don't need this shit."
"Can't I just…see how you live for today?"
"What, no! Piss off like your buddy did, my community service is done for the day!"

She grabbed hold of my arm and pleaded even more desperately now. This is getting pathetic, and not to mention that she is causing a scene in public also. Too exhausted to care at this point…and too exhausted to have her committed. 'A fan of my work', wait until T hears about this lunacy. Better yet, it is best not to; might slit her throat just from having physical contact with me if I disavowed her touch.

Dice roll for the new ronin.

"Jesus Christ fine, but I recorded your words so don't try some kidnapped or rape scenario to the cops. How old are you anyway?"
"Eighteen…"
"…No more talking because I'm starting to think you and trouble are siblings."

2005 vs. 2021…I hate where this is going already. Seeing Anthony's relations with women, along with my own, have always pointed to women being the precursors to some terrible events ready to unfold…but we love to gamble still.

Base is not far off; best get my driver to pick us up to avoid more stares.

A soft expression grew on her while wiping away at her cheeks. Best to keep a close eye on this one, god knows how damaged her psyche is. The false eye noticed her calm composure; cortisol levels decreased and heart rate nominal…but it also noticed quick glances at me every so often before averting her sights to the ground. My only reaction was to grin.

I would be lying if I said it was not cute, but she might get me killed also…surprises come in all forms, eh mother?

W.L. woods hid sanctuary: a small building where several other members lived with my permission. The vicinity held various secrets that I withheld from the bosses in case a scenario like this were to happen, and with secrets comes a multitude of protection: hidden barriers to bug sized sentries. Lady Cosme's personal orbiter still has not penetrated through, thanks to a certain "ally" nearby.

These woods hide more danger than we button men do.

Do not go too deep inside unless you are infatuated with silver brides encased in a brown casket amongst camouflaged graves. Your reception will consist of nothing, but the chattering of voltaic automatons taunting your struggle to break free.

"I always heard that this area was protected by God's force to prevent the Eden inside to be soiled. They even did a story about this on the news where getting a satellite picture was impossible. You really are the real thing!" she said in amazement.

"What? Do you hear yourself talk?" I replied shaking my head.

Her eyes bounced to all sides…I wonder if there are any marbles ricocheting off each other. Is it deception or did her naivety really ensure her survival up to this point?

Approaching the entrance, an intercom let out a short feedback.

"Who's the girl?" a digital voice said.

Enter Mr. P.S.

"She's a star-struck fan of the underground circuit; my personal guest."
"…How many nerve cells did you lose facing Valentine? No go, she needs to leave. The bosses think she's just a piece of ass, but we both know T wouldn't allow a liability to walk in here."

I guess the tabs have started…

"I'm feeling risky today; I'll talk to T about this. Don't forget who's in charge here."

"...Fine Mr. Personality, but she's out the second I hear trouble."

The reinforced door opened slowly. More amazement grew on her face when she saw the technology and automated weapons throughout the hallway. Surprised, T herself did not become the welcome party. Ten to one she is planning something to use against me. My guess are those long legs of hers to knock me sideways...and maybe put out her 'curves' to pasture. The elevators in sight, top floor now before she has time to react.

"No way," she said upon exiting the cage.

Paralysis took hold of her very being. The sudden sight of twin behemoth automatons, beside my home entrance, would cause a sense of dread at first glance.

"Password," they asked with booming voices.

The 'inner workings' inside me had healed most of the damage to my throat. Pronunciation was the key to voice recognition; else, a torrent of violence would shred me to pieces.

"Leto is Mother. Nyx is Daughter. Nephthys is Lover."

The automatons opened the door without hesitation and now stood directly in front of the entrance after our entry. From wonder, to fear, it seemed confusion now struck the face of this nubile.

What will your next color of expression be from the palette?

"You have technology that surpasses any other, but you have such a mundane apartment. I don't get it," she said still looking around.

The candor leaving her lips made my palette choose the 'color' of exasperation. Maybe I am giving her too much credit; naivety was never attractive to me. This tour might be a lot shorter than I expected it to be. Perhaps something more interesting will spruce up the conversation if I exhibit le jardin out back.

A tent concealed the makeshift area; it was there she saw my own little Eden, which contained a small lab, several giant bamboos, and a nest. The curious bunny approached the empty nest wondering its purpose. Good thing she is a bit dim because 'he' has his sights on her, and it has been a while since he played with another...

"Hey, do you have an animal living here?"
"..."
"Eddy?" she asked again turning to me.

She noticed I was staring upwards behind her, but it was too late to evade. The creature had pounced onto her back and screams emitted loudly. The very depths of her being thought death fell upon her when really...it was holding onto dear life.

Shaking the creature off her back, it ran up to my shoulder to wrap its arms around my neck. I tried keeping a straight face as one could possibly withstand. Laughing would be too cruel now…her heart rate needed to slow down before a stroke ensued.

"It's a golden bamboo lemur."

Finally catching her breath, she fixed her disheveled look; glasses half off. Something about the look quickly disarmed my jesting…my veins felt extra sensitive…

"Why didn't you say something? Oh my god…"
"I guess he wanted a bigger snack than from the branches above your head."

Her eyes twitched at me, it was plain as day to see that look of annoyance. I guess there is a bit of fight in her after all.

"I never pegged you for an animal person, considering your living arrangements."
"The point of my living conditions is simple: I was never inflicted with the poison known as materialism. Also…I don't have the most advanced tech. What you see is all on loan."
"I didn't mean to offend you if that's what you think…just…surprised is all."

She approached me now, a bit cautiously, but smiled when I was being playful with the lemur. He gnawed on my finger and looked at her with his wide hazel eyes.

"I'm not sure I understand, you're saying you own none of these things, on what...credit?"

"While my pleasures are basic from the suits to cigars there are a few complexes to everyone's persona. My associates and I have a sort of fetish for defensive/offensive technology. We believe that no one person is safe from anything and so we rather try to win a losing game of checkers against God. When we all began our research for the 'best defense', we started with plenty of raw material and funds. However, the drawback was simply networking. We are death dealers so trust is the hardest commodity to come by. It took a long time to gain a foothold with those in technology; namely because we had to deal with governmental espionage, selfish greedy startups, etc. One of my superiors, if you will, has various crowning achievements that have saved our hides numerous times. However, we realized there was a threat located in a Republic of Scandinavia. I personally took care of it a few years ago, but destroyed most of the work except one...for personal reasons. My superior was not happy, but they will understand one day...or not. Now than before I continue I just need to know one thing."

I leaned my torso over her body now. She did not know how to react besides having her pale skin flush red. Her eyes were so...familiar.

"Who the hell are you?"

She lowered her eyes again to the floor. I knew she was nervous and I took the initiative. Placing my hand under her chin, her face began to rise once more.

"Averting the eyes can lead to lies and deceit. Two sets of portals, connecting with each other, open windows to the true user's aura. Thus, silver tongues from rogues can even pour truths themselves. There is no need to be nervous as I am very eager to learn about a so called 'fan' of mine."

Ears must be playing tricks on me…I swear I heard a faint moan escape. Do not use the eye to cheat if there is perspiration down below!

"…Blue, just…Blue: adopted. Mom died giving birth to me…and dad took his life because of it; all I know is that I was born somewhere in Nuevo León. Friends' of his got me over on this side of the line somehow. However, HSI caught them in the process, stranding me here. Lady who calls herself 'mom' is never around, and 'dad'…rather not say. It was five years ago when I started to notice you and your brother in the news. I thought you were some deranged criminal who escaped an insane asylum, from what the news showed, but I saw the leaked video of you in China. You and Anthony saved all those lives! You…" she continued.

An asylum…THE asylum…I don't see the Shepherd anymore, but…

"Enough!" I interrupted her.

She yelped and stared at me with further confusion.

"I am not a messenger of God, and I am not some wanna-be vigilante. I am a hot-blooded misanthrope who enjoys venting to earn his keep. Despite the news regarding the pardon, or anything else they spout with a half-baked mindset, I still hold my blade against any. Do not make me a Saint." I continued, "This conversation is over and I hope you enjoyed being this close to me without being killed, but now it's time for you to kindly piss off."

Her eyes were wide and I could see them turn red a bit. She wanted to cry, but held it in. I should have known better, this was a mistake.

Taking her quickly outside of the forest, I had one of my associates give her a ride home. It cannot be helped mom; I just can't allow her to get close. I did not even let T get this close back in Europe!

Blue looked at me through the car window and started to tear up. Her lips quivered and she clenched her eyes tightly. She proceeded to pull out a small case from her bag; glasses placed inside, and looked at me one more time before the car drove off. Absolute dread fell on me...how did I not see something this goddamn simple! My neck stiffened slightly once she was out of sight. She was the visage of Venus who pierced my throat from the nightmare!

Without hesitation, I phoned my associate to put a button camera on her bag. My watch told me it was 5:31 and dusk was starting to set in; an intervention with fate needed to be prepared.

● ● ●

A new journal will have her name engraved into it...

"Can you tell Eddy I didn't mean to offend him...please?" Blue said to the driver.
"Of course, here's a tissue."

Blowing her nose, he placed the camera on her person. Exiting, without a hint of realization, Blue entered the small apartment building she called 'home'.

"You were supposed to be here three hours ago. Where have you been Blue?" a lecherous man said standing by the doorway.
"Nowhere, I just wanted to go for a walk."
"Now why don't I believe that?" he said getting closer to her.

He started smelling her around the neck.

"Cologne? I thought I was the only man in your life?"
"It was one of my friends, nothing more. Can I go in now?" she said looking at the floor.
"Of course no one's stopping you. Your mom won't be home for a bit so how 'bout cooking naked this time, eh?"

Through his grimace look, a small touch of drool showed itself from the corner of his chapped mouth. She was not able to stomach his smile: receding gums and piss stained bones. The visualization of halitosis traced from his raspy voice. A quick rush to her small room, followed by a forecast of showers began in silence. Venus collapsed on the ground trying to muffle her cries.

It was now I started to weigh in the pros and cons. After a few hours of observing the camera, I made my decision on her life. My driver was given instructions for the morning, and I continued to observe the monitor a little longer than I should have. A faint shiver ran through my spine…the "Huntress" fell on me.

"What have we here, I never pegged you for voyeurism?"

"…Where've you been Tanya?" my eyes still facing ahead.

"Talking to Smith regarding the news between you and Anthony. Once I saw him let you in with that snow bunny, I figured it best to watch from afar and do a bit of thinking."

"Thinking what exactly?"

Now a pair of arms was thrown from behind me, one caressing the chest and the other against my neck. Her mouth against my right ear, it had higher sensitivity from the surgery.

"I was wondering if you were planning to have tryst in your penthouse with her."

Her doting arms were tightening up. A wrong answer might get you killed old boy.

ARMOUR

"Sympathy only for the broken animal, call it a hunch, but I think she might be a good addition...politically wise at least."

"Are you bored of me? Do you think I'm that dumb?" her voice trembled.

"...I'm so tired of the old ways T; I'm betting a pretty innocent face like hers will do us right in the public eye. If I am to bring any sort of peace, I must begin to employ talents of virtue. Here, take a copy of the footage and judge for yourself if you think she deserves this. Leave me alone now, and for the record...I could never get bored of you."

"My little sage forgets: You can't bring peace if you're still in war. The bosses are impatient..."

Her teeth bit into my lobe and a flick of the tongue soothed the pain, one of my weaknesses. With a copy taken from me, she left as quickly as she came. If Paris did not harm our relationship, then the Shepherd was the one to kill it...

My 72-hour reply was to be in effect at 12am and I have never felt this nauseous since the asylum contract. Maybe the mirror will ease me for once; some facial tissue still required healing, but merely for molding appearance. A huge feat is almost ending. It was best to leave the scars on my body; a reminder I too can bleed and die. However, I want my original face again: no room for error, and no limit to expenses. She will see it one day...maybe, but for now, I rest.

Her life belongs to me.

New horizons bring in the endless change. Some curse the day at birth of the sun while others greet it with warm lending hands. On this day, both will occur…carnography will revel amongst the lamb. Call it a test to see how much of a 'fan' you really are…

Blue rose from her bed and made her way to the bathroom: paste on the brush and a yawn from the lungs.

"…Mine." a voice echoed behind her.

She turned quickly and noticed no one was there. Making her way to the brightly lit living room, she noticed her father tied to a chair with a bit in his mouth. Her eyes noticed me sitting with my head down in front him and two masked associates standing by his sides. Panic set in and she backed away slowly. I rose up and turned to her.

"Easy now, sit on the couch."

I nodded to my associates to release the bit.

"You mummified faggot! You can't do this! The cops will get right on your ass again! I'm untouchable!"

"So angry, look at how you fluster!" I replied.

I went behind him and placed my hands on his shoulders.

"How long have you been naughty to Blue?"

"I don't need to answer you!"

"Evading the question will earn you a punishment. Not asking again…"

"Fuck you ghoulie!"

I grinned and noticed the window fan behind me.

"Not summer and you have the window fan still in the frame. Let's use it for other means shall we."

The fan was taken out and the window was closed immediately. Certain sounds must be drowned.

"Close the curtains." I said to an associate.
"What're you going to do dumb ass? Cut my hands off with a barely fast piece of plastic crap." He said laughing at me.
"No, but it's good to know you still have a brain to know what a fan is. No, I'm not going to cut off your hands. It would take too long and the most damage I can do is small bruises to your wrists. What I'm about to do with this simple harmless looking junk is much more rewarding."

I violently ripped the cover off along with the plastic blade and tossed them to the ground. The fan was switched to the highest setting now.
"While the blade was harmless the metal prod that spins it is bound to do damage. Notice how it's heating up nicely. Tell me, have you heard the phrase 'eye for an eye'? Now, if you want to keep your eyes intact you will give me your daughter to adopt as my own. Do you agree? Or does the latter suit you more?" I said with my right eye glowing underneath the bandages.

"Fine she's yours! Do whatever you want with her! Let me go!" he screamed.

"You're so quick to give an answer. Blue I want you to pack your essentials now. The rest will be picked up at a later time." I said handing the fan to an associate.

"I'm calling the cops the second I get a chance you shit head!"

"The cops are the ones to provide me evidence of your past deeds. If I were to give them the video of you hitting on your daughter, along with several children from the area, it will put you away for some time. I know you are the reason for her post-traumatic stress disorder. Be happy I'm letting you live...with a remembrance of me of course." I said licking the upper row of my teeth.

My associate stood in front of him with the fan still on.

"I thought you said you weren't going to kill me!"

"Of course I'm not going to. I can't ruin my newfound freedom, can I? However, the cops will turn a 'blind eye' to the situation. Get it?" I said laughing.

"Would like to watch this Blue?" I said to her.

She shook her head without saying a word.

"I can understand. The first is usually the worst to swallow. Why don't you go listen to some music in your room while we finish in here? Oh and do you have some salt? Oh never mind, there's a thermometer right here on the wall. No need to worry he will still be alive after I use this. I'm a very careful individual…with only a few fatal accidents." I said turning around to face him.

She immediately went in her room and started blasting the music. His screams were drowned out, but he provided much of a mess. The eyeball spewed fluids and the prod caused it to become entangled: a swift ejection across the floorboards.

His screams were mute, but I could practically see down his esophagus. Breaking the glass tube over his bare socket, a few droplets of the mercury trickled in. Comatose settled in from the living nightmare and needed to react quickly. From the kitchen, an ice cube was pulled out from the freezer tray. Pulling his head back, I dropped the small iceberg in place. A quick shot to the brain jolted him awake. Time was of the essence now to wrap this up. We needed to cauterize the wound so...we shot a few bullets into his hands and placed the barrel of the gun directly inside the socket. He screamed again, but still muted and passed out once more.

"Shall we dispose of him sir?"

"Unfortunately we cannot, he's not worth the ass hairs of my crack."

"He'll definitely die from this kind of infection soon though..."

"Christ, set a healer on him, but leave behind a yellow jacket just in case he phones this in."

"...Yes sir."

The eye sensed an irritation in their mannerisms. Could a mutiny be in the works?

I went to Blue's door and put my arm inside, trying my best to signal her to turn the music off, but to no avail. Taking it upon myself to enter the room, I noticed she was in her brassiere with her back to me. Quickly turning off the music, the door was shut with great force. The twins in my chest exhaled deeply, thinking to myself: all the fat must go to the chest.

Further directions were made for my associates and they waited outside the apartment. It was not long before we all left the property. Although to my bewilderment, Blue did not scream or wince at the grisly sight left behind. She just…stared shortly and left just as easily. I cannot tell if this now became a charity or a Christmas gift to her.

I misjudged her…
"Um, did you turn off...?"
"No time for talk we have to go now." I interrupted her.

We looked outside the building carefully and waited for a few people to pass by. When it was clear, we entered the car and drove off calmly. I stared outside the window; heart pounding excessively. For the first time in almost five years, I was actually nervous again. A bit of lost adolescence still lingers in me I suppose.

"How does Anthony do it?" I said to myself.
"Sir?"
"Never mind, I'm just mumbling to myself. Let's get back to base ASAP."

Peripheral vision noticed Blue staring at her lap. I guess this was a little too sudden to take in all at once, but I refused to let a stranger from my dream pass me by without me knowing their exact standing in my life.

A restricted number called my phone…this is how trouble starts…

"Where's the specter wire?" I asked my associates.
"Glove compartment sir."

The trace was being made once attached; there were no words, but the sounds of heavy breathing.

"…" my ear hearing a familiar sound, then the exchanges started.
"I'm coming for you," a robotic voice said.
"It's not even the afternoon and a 'King of Goats' is causing my face to flush."
"Joke all you want. It..."
"...won't save me? Apparently, it has all these years. Either talk like a human or I can mail you a doodle on a napkin."
"You opened up a weak spot Roman. I'd never figure you for having a bit of the complex. Is she the Haze to your Humbert? Don't worry, I won't reveal the torture video to the 'proper' authorities, but you have to meet me so we can close this little deal."
"Not interested." I replied hanging up.

The trace revealed the pervasive caller: under the car.

"Problems sir?" the driver asked.

"When is there never one? Hit the gas quickly, we have a leech underneath us."

"What! Shouldn't we get out?" Blue shouted.

The eye showed that most of the floor was reinforced, except for a few spots…

"Get your feet up Blue, now!"
"Why?"

A serrated blade pierced through between her feet.

"That's why…"

Her scrambling was breaking my concentration. The eye showed her hands going for the seatbelt. I screamed at her not to release the switch, and another attack from below commenced. Now she was screaming…this won't be good if this drags out. Wait…drags out.

"Make a sharp turn into this complex lot!" I commanded my driver.

With the headstrong speed we were going, blood from all parties are about to be spilled. The vehicle nearly ejected us through the windshield, and the airbags kicked in from the impact. Everything came to a full stop. I was the first out of the car, disregarding the bloodied nose.

The lots speed bump revealed blood, but no body. This is impossible! The blood trails a few feet…and just stops. The eye searched voraciously for any hints. My associates stumbled out with Blue. Something is not right here; an unusual breeze flowing past me.

"Eddy...I don't feel good..." Blue groggily said.

Blood trickled down the side of her face. The sight caused an unusual rage to build up...must calm down!

"Get her back inside!" I screamed with the knife extracted.

The associate stopped halfway before the impossible revealed itself. His body levitated a few inches off the ground and he started to make choking sounds. I could see the impression of a hand gripping his throat, and yet...I could not see the hand! His flesh ripped off and blood saturated into the veins of broken concrete. The second pulled out his gun to shoot about blindly.

"Idiot, we're in plain sight! Hold before you shoot a passerby!"

As another breeze was rushing by, he turned to me to reveal a hole in his head before collapsing. Faint laughter could be heard around us. Not good, the eye can't pinpoint this ghost.

"Eddy..."

She was on one knee now, hand reaching out to me. My driver trying to make sense of the situation walked slowly towards her.

"Don't move!" I yelled at him.

I need assistance from another source. They were always close to me in dire situations, the eye made contact with them. Nearby birds flew away upon their arrival. Neon red sprites buzzing around the vicinity like fireflies. A great gamble to reveal them so openly…

The eye picked up unusual kinetics from the wind. The breeze was moving towards Blue! The laughing happened again. Blue looked around with sweat and blood running down together.

Mother, please guide me…

The eye signaled the sprites to her position. The sounds of buzzing was heard from them, and a small hurricane of red surrounded her.

"Goddammit!" a voice screamed out from behind her.

In that brief moment, a face revealed itself. He had his own companions attached to his body…so this is your secret to invisibility.

"Subdue!" I commanded, pointing at him.

The crimson will-o-wisps started to carve about at his vicinity. This presented an opening to get to Blue. More parts of him were unveiled with each slice from their tiny saws and stingers. My driver taking this opportunity to help turn the tide. He tossed over a flash-bang to me.

"Enough!" the assassin screamed.

He knocked out the driver and pushed through the sprites towards us. Pulling Blue to me, I told her to hold tightly. Extending the free arm out to a nearby tree, the lunatic was bull-rushing with such velocity. That enormous serrated knife was so close that our reflections were as clear as day.

Blue looked at my body and saw it moving; the cranking of gears initiated. A shot ejected from the sleeve and the device pulled us off the ground. Thank god for this harpoon system because his knife literally held a faint impression in the air; so fast. My left shoulder cracked from slamming into the trunk. How many times will I fix these rotator cuffs?

Screams could be heard, and towards us nonetheless. His momentum did not hinder at all from our evasion. Hail Mary…

"Close your eyes and cross your fingers," I said to Blue.

Her soft body clenched to me, a nice way to die…

Once more, his knife high above with the knuckles more white than before.

Closing my eyes, a huge burst emitted before him. The flash-bang went off midair, both blinding him and causing all the skittering components to disperse from his body. His pupils resembled the surrounding sclera. Enough was right, and now I stood before him. He swung about violently trying to make a connection. More gears under the suit, but deeper below. The right hand caught his knife and cracked it off the hilt.

"But how!" he yelled.

Secrets from the past…an unforeseen blessing from Valentine…

Bringing my right arm back, a deadly connection of my fist and his chest came to be; cracked sternum reporting for duty. He gasped and dropped like stone.

"Fucking hell…" I sighed looking at my associates who were once breathing.
"…Sir…we have to go…" my driver said with a weak voice.

The sirens were not far off. The damaged car was still operative for a getaway thankfully. Blue was unresponsive now…shit. Laying her in the back, I had my other 'companions' descend upon her. Green sprites emitted their rays on her injuries. My driver and I threw the ghost man into the trunk, and now became ghosts from the scene.

● ● ●

From the trees overlooking the lot were unseen mechanical eyes. The event that unfolded transmitted to other parties unbeknownst to us.

"Seems like it failed." A female's voice said.

"Your upgrades will definitely compromise us now..." another female said to the first.

"So let's call in the chin beard to finish the job!" a male stated.

"What makes you think he is capable?" the first female asked.

"You've seen firsthand N's subjects reaction to his drugs..." he responded.

"After all these years of loving him, and the others, we just end up as strangers again." The second female said.

"...Call in our UC's and tell them we're not doing the 72-hour reply anymore. With Smith and Tanya rejecting our offers...it's so hard to say goodbye." The first female said.

"They made their choice, get 'money bags' from Dolore Tech on the line." The male demanded from a nearby associate.

With the trio calling in the fourth, a new world order was in the works...and it started with a sinner known as, "The Meprodine."

"Let me out!" the assassin yelled from the trunk.

"Do we have any more of the gas?" I asked my driver.

"I'll deploy some now sir," he responded.

A faint hissing sound went off inside the trunk from a press of a button on the wheel.

"How're you feeling?" I asked Blue.

"Better, what are these things?" she asked looking at the floating sprites.

Putting my finger out one landed on top. Her weary eyes saw the true shape of it.

"Is that...an insect?"

"Only by shape, these automatons are known as healers: spined soldier bugs. The ones protecting you before are our offensive yellow jackets, and our spies...they're around too, just look for your color."

"Another company secret?"

"...How would you like a permanent residency?"

"Is this another test?"

"No, I'm short on time to play games. Deception is never something I put on my subordinates, how could I expect honesty from them? This offer comes with every basic human need, and an allowance. Politics need to be addressed and we need a new image. Anthony's people can set you up with that portion; mine will oversee your safety."

"Does he know about me?"

"Possibly...possibly not, but your decision needs to be said now. If you refuse, I have already prepared a large transaction into your checking account. I have also obtained a valid passport to be used because I do not suggest staying in this country, at the moment, if you object to my offer: too many variables to explain."

Home base in sight and the look on her face made it seem Russian roulette was a safer choice.

"So, you could stay in the car to be driven to JFK or...welcome home," I said getting out.

Strange winter this has become and a more peculiar way to end the year. I have to remind myself that I'm not trying to fix this girl, I'm simply lending aid and looking for assistance to this manmade island. She's not entirely damaged goods, but I've never once had a dream felt so vivid and real. Surreal is what it is. Maybe she reminds me of you mom. Maybe she reminds me of Leila in the dream or maybe...

...I'm just over fucking analyzing and should leave it up to fate whether she will be the one to bring my empire down. Maybe I just don't care anymore, and retirement with a bullet to the heart is a better way to exit.

A frozen icicle dropped from a nearby tree to bring me back. I didn't realize Blue was standing next to me. That look of concern...someone could have killed me a thousand times over right now. The frost isn't the only thing to make me catatonic.

"If this is your decision, then so be it. Stay here for a few, need to make a call inside. No eavesdropping allowed." I continued, "He's not going to like this one bit..."

Tony's persona is not one to welcome foreigners who weren't vetted properly, but this is my side of the pond so my fucking rules. However, if it's within his grasp, he'll erase it immediately. Testosterone levels are higher than usual. The keyword for this conversation is indifference.

"Eddy, have you decided to take that trip up north?" Tony said on the phone.

"No, but something came across my desk this time…"

After what appeared to be a lifetime a decision was made: brother is coming for a stern visit.

My phone was the one to ring now. I wanted to ignore it, seeing just how it was from base, but I proceeded.

"Talk to me."

"Eddy we have a big problem!" an associate said on the other end.

"One of Dolore Tech's drones is closing in on our location. ETA is 4 minutes!"

4 minutes, is everyone getting new tech except for me? What is Laurent doing sending one of his toys to my residence without a formal warning?

"Get Laurent on the line and ask him what his company's doing by sending a drone in our vicinity. That's an order!"

"That's the thing! He's currently having a meeting with the bosses! It's another negotiation between the four of them. System defenses are booting up right now. I'm marking you and the others for clearance through the woods."

"I have two players in the car that are ID'ed as pedestrian. I need a pass for just one of them while the other is being transferred to the facility." I said looking at my watch.

"No go."

"What do you mean 'no go'? It's the girl I took on tour yesterday!"

"Some teenagers within the general area are loitering and considering we didn't expect this to happen we left it alone instead of making ourselves visible. I'm sorry."

"How far out are they?" I asked feverishly.

"Not too far from the wheat field."

"Send some of the spies on them. If they don't budge after that then release the yellow jackets."

Must be amateur hour today, this is too sloppy. Christ, being halfway between base and Blue, I forgot about his lechery! A virgin, a mummy, and a dog in heat walk into a bar…

My driver decided to stretch his feet outside, Blue joined him.

"Will everything be alright?" Blue asked.

"Mr. Roman doesn't handle pressure well, but still manages…he has no choice. You saw how he was in the parking lot. That is his normal. Why don't we start unpacking your belongings now, he usually doesn't keep guests waiting for long."

Blue waited next to the car, many thoughts running through her head. Was this the best decision?

"Why hello there hermosa." a man said to Blue.

The driver dropped one of her bags to the ground. Elder brother arrived in place of a drone, and he was leaning in on Blue.

"My dear you have a very unique smell. Did you know that?"

She did not reply, a cold sweat started to produce.

"You smell like...Tahitian vanilla. While I prefer Aztec chocolate, your pheromones are simply delicious. Might I acquire your name?"

Upgrades were not limited to just limbs you know.

"Mr. Ro..." my driver said.
"I'm not talking to you, am I?" Anthony interrupted.
A swift punch to the gut laid him out; once a pugilist, always a pugilist.

"I'm sorry you had to see that my dear. Name please?" he asked again.
"Eddy!" Blue screamed at the top of her lungs.

Anthony raised his brow in confusion when he heard this. Wide were his eyes upon hearing a faint piercing sound coming in his direction. He flew his head backward just missing a dart to the chin. Blue began running to the forest immediately, but the elder grabbed hold of her.

"That's enough Eddy why don't you come out now!"

I exited the forest without my blazer and had my sleeves rolled up.

"I haven't seen that look in quite some time. You mind explaining why a commoner is beckoning you so easily. Is THIS what you were telling me about?" Anthony asked while holding Blue back.

"I can explain."

"Please do!"

Our quarrel had been interrupted however with the faint sounds of bashing. Anthony turned his attention to the car trunk and picked the lock. The assassin rose his head up immediately and tried escaping. Brother pulled out a stun gun and released a surge of electricity into his chest. As he yelled in pain, Anthony slammed the trunk down on his head knocking him out. He stared at me with a poker face.

"Care to explain this also?" he yelled.

"...Just another bump in the road."

"I can never tell if you're joking or being serious, but apparently we need to have a goddamn sit down now you little pretentious shit!"

Blue was behind me holding onto my shoulders and cowering her head. He began to walk quickly to me and grabbed one of my hands to sniff.

"Sangre." he said to me in a stern voice.

Before I could react, he put his hand up to my face and shook his head. I knew he did not want to hear about it now until we were in a more private area. Smelling salts were given to my driver.

"You need to respect my men at least..." I said, with the eye blinding him.

Brushing him off, instructions were given to phone into the facility about the ghost and to hold him there for 'interrogation'. With my sights on Tony and Blue, I realized a disastrous new chapter had just begun.

Good...

"I think we've got enough evidence to prove they didn't change," an undercover officer said to his partner.

More variables watching from afar.
"The captain will be happy to hear about this. Let's get this over to the precinct ASAP." his partner said.
"Let me call in base first to see what they want to do about this." the first cop said.

Trying to radio dispatch, silence had greeted the duo. Frustration was mounting when even their cellphones were inoperative. The 'Stoic' intervenes...

"Car 17, remove yourselves from the premises now. We know who you are and where your families live. Leave now before they identify as a 10-45D. Is that understood or would you prefer zip locks to a coffin?"

The static resumed and the dispatcher became clear once more. "Car 17...10-9?" the dispatcher asked.
"...Nothing to report base." he replied lowly.
"Fucking Roman's." the second officer said.

First and last, NYPD wipeout occurred thirteen years ago. If you are going to make history, a semi and a fire hydrant is an innovative way to do it.

An argument ensued inside the walls of the safe house.

"Please tell me she's some sort of scapegoat for a past affair you forgot to take care of!" Anthony shouted at me.

It was rare to see him away from his calm manner. All associates had their doors locked, but I am sure their ears were pressed.
"I've been planning this for so long Eddy I forget what time is sometimes. Why? Why!"
"Intueri..."
"Intuition! Did uncle hit you with some of his psychological 'find yourself' paradox? Why don't we all just start brainstorming right now! Sure lets set the problem! Then we will split it into components and create a perfectly definite question! Next, we will invite your bosses, as well as mine, together to discuss and create a list

of leads! Finally, we'll come to some sort of solution and celebrate by drinking Tieguanyin tea because we finally found out what the FUCK makes you tick sometimes!"

My ears began to blister. Blue was still behind me keeping close and quiet.

"What're you going to tell me next? That you'll teach her to be your 3rd?" he said sarcastically.
"Course not. I don't plan to put her in the fire."

Anthony sighed and turned around.

"Good. That's very good." he said peacefully.
"At least not now…"

He quickly turned around and shot a bullet into my chest.

"Eddy!" Blue began to scream.
"Quiet! Death doesn't come easily for him." He said holstering his pistol.
"It…still….hurts though." I groaned out.

Blue began to open up my shirt to examine me. Upon further examination, she noticed I had a thin protective vest on me. A sigh of relief was released from her. This time the words to come to mind were Dopamine and Norepinephrine. I looked at Anthony and he simply shook his head; a sadistic smile came with it. He knelt and extended his sometimes "olive branch". Blue, however, smacked it away. His smile disappeared and was about to slap her. With pure instinct, the right arm gripped it. The banshee left his mouth.

"Truce goddammit!"

The eye picked up his hand's deformities: hairlines in the phalanges and metacarpals, and all were broken surrounding the capitate.

"It's been a while since we fought hasn't it?" he said.

Personal healers came to his aid to perform the surgery.

"Fine, but she's your responsibility. Don't cry on me if your pet dies on you prematurely."

Sleeves unrolled now.

"What's her name at least?"
"Blue. No last name."
"Elle s'appelles Bleu? Maybe one day you will adopt the Roman name as a sister. But seeing as my brother has an interest in you, which is a rare case, you'll probably adopt it for some other reason."
"…Can we get on with more important matters?"
"Fine, let's go visit your place for a bit. It's been a while since I've seen your little lemur friend," he replied heading for the elevator.
"Stay down here for a bit. This shouldn't take long." I said to Blue before walking away.

She extended her hand a bit as if trying to reach for me. Still assessing the crazed situation, that we call normal, it was in her best interest to stand by quietly and remain composed. A loud clank came from behind her; more surprises for her? One of the apartment doors opened up slowly. Tanya emerged and crossed her arms; predator before prey. Her eyes analyzed the young Venus…and bit down on her lip.

"So…you're Edward's new pet project?"

Blue did not answer her, but only to step back.

"You are just the cutest thing. Beautiful green eyes, long black hair, full lips, a bit top heavy, and beautifully pale skin. Even your glasses add a nice detail to that cute face of yours. You are so skittish too. What do you say you come inside while you wait for him? He may be prompt with timing, but his brother leaves much to be desired sometimes for a clean-cut playboy." she said while taking Blues hands.

"That's ok. I can just wait out here. The atmosphere isn't all that bad."
"Don't be so modest little one. I'll take good care of you," she said pulling Blue inside.

Her inhuman strength caught Blue by surprise; the Dokkaebi must have possessed Tanya I sometimes thought. The apartment door closed and the loud clanks of the locks were heard once more.

● ● ●

A quick rush to the refrigerator as my throat was very dry considering the circumstances. A few homebrewed vials for me, and one for Tony. Healers need to charge sometime. Without saying anything, we quickly shot down the elixirs.

"Eddy...you and I both know I leave your personal life alone unless need be. However, we do not need this type of shit. It's been less than a day since we've had our shackles released. You cannot have her here; remember how your last two infatuations went before you joined? One had you thrown to jail without defending you, and the last one was the worst. A twelve-year investment and she left you for dead without so much as a goodbye because we found her fucking everyone on the block. Don't you remember when her crazy parents went off on you? Those "bloodcleets" were begging you to die. Just imagine how this would play out if you lost her, especially if this goes into the long run again."

With my head hanging low, I could just visualize the sword of Damocles above me.

"I saw her in a dream Anthony. I just cannot explain now at the moment. I saw how her upbringing was as well. The abuse she was taking...sure I thought emotionally, but her 'dad' needed a lesson. Ours just left, not before that incident with the beer. Mom tried to raise us right, but the damn country just had to increase healthcare...again. And where the fuck was uncle in all this? Nowhere, and then of all things to claim her was a goddamn jar of peanut butter containing salmonella. She just smiled when she heard about the recall. "At least no one else will get sick," she said. She just kept smiling until the last moment. Finally, he shows up after the fact. Zero explanation for absence, and we were never told anything about him until a few weeks after she died. Getting back to the point, I feel I should have her examined by Uncle. Maybe he can shed some light on my interest in her."

Anthony crossed his arms and smirked.

"Alright, I can respect that, despite being overly dramatic. As I said though, she's your responsibility. Training her will be a challenge though. She's just reaching adulthood and has the mind of a timid saint. If she's interested in you though that might leave a hint of possible talent. Any idea how smart she is?"

"Can't say, but you and I both know that women have a better reach at knowledge than men."

"And that is why dear brother, smart women will always be our shared love," he replied with a grin.

It was time to reconvene with Blue, but when we exited the elevator, she was nowhere around.

"There's only a few players in the building which apartment do you think she went into?" Anthony asked.

He began to sniff the air. It still baffles me we could enhance our basic senses nowadays. Goddamn bloodhound, you can't make this shit up sometimes.

"The aroma is a bit refreshing all of a sudden. Perfume would be my guess. Uh-oh…she's been ensnared by the competition." He said laughing.

Christ, when did life start becoming a Spanish soap?

Looking at T's door, I made an executive decision to kick it open. Upon entering the apartment, a woman was giggling in the background.

Life transitions: happy, sad, anger, repulsed, more anger, anguish, indifferent, and now…comedy.

When we entered the living room, we noticed Tanya standing over Blue, exposing her bra and panties, while she was in her birthday suit. Brother was enjoying this view more than I was.

Need to manage better…

"Why is it Tanya that you don't ever play with me like this?" he asked studying her body.

She threw a hidden blade from her hair towards him. His quick reflexes caught the handle in time. Ever so close to the nose.

"Another time perhaps…I'll send word to my people, there's nothing to report now. Remember, you and me need to discuss this Valentine case next time, but I'm late for my meeting with you-know-who. In addition, I have been hearing little birds talking about the police trying something new to get us gone now. Best to play hermit for a little while until either of us get better intel on the matter. I'll be taking my leave now, oh…regarding her 'father',

I'm having cleaners sent over. I'm getting tired of cleaning up after you, but what're big brothers for. Have fun with your new family Blue." Anthony said, making his exit.

"Tanya…what was the plan here, had I arrived at a later time?"

She went from all fours to a kneeling position and turned her head to me.

"Why not take advantage of the situation? Two women and one man is nothing short than a fantasy is it not?"

She crawled to my legs and grabbed onto my belt. Don't sweat the details now, this is for another tale.

"Carpe Diem amour." She said looking up to me.
Never give into sex unless you know in detail who you are fucking…less problems in the future.
With a small push, she became startled. I crouched before her and began to pet her hair softly; only I could get away with this. Closing her eyes, a little disappointed smile told me she understood. I kissed her forehead to show her I never mean to be intentionally cruel. I'm still not ready to surrender when chaos still runs amok.

"Not now, but maybe one day kitten. Clarity is with me these days, as opposed to last year. Blue whenever you're done with getting acquainted with the floor, I need you to come with me."

Tanya collapsed on the floor and sighed deeply.

"Hate when he does that. Maybe if he was gay or even bi I'd accept his rejections more easily."

She noticed Blue from the corner of her eyes trying to make a quick escape. Tanya leaped up and grasped Blue from behind.

"I may be his pet, but soon you'll be mine." She said whispering to her ear.

She bit it a little before releasing her. Blue yelped and ran out the door. I looked inside and winked at T before closing the door.

"Let's proceed now shall we?" I said heading to the elevator.

She was breathing heavily once we entered.

"I'm sure you're wondering what a phenomenon like that is doing with a cast of shades."

She looked up to me with curious eyes.

"Well, I can't tell you that, it's not my place. You're just going to have to ask her yourself. I will give you one tip though: Domination. Think of it as one of your first tests in conquering the human mind and bending its will to however you shape it."

The elevator opened to the middle floor.

"Welcome to your new life of burdens…!"

She passed out again; I thought she healed properly from before? The right arm again reacted before I could. Does V have remote control? Venus' face was before mine now.

"Oxytocin…vasopressin…what the hell's wrong with me?" I said struggling to get her inside the apartment.

Gently as possible, her body laid down on the couch. Lesser men would think criminally at this point.

"You're going to be my greatest challenge, aren't you?"
A blank apartment and already I was curious as to how she would customize it. Before taking my leave, I left her a note on the kitchen counter. Closing the door, several underlings had approached me. They all stared at me with frigid eyes, except one: my right-hand Piotr Smith, The Stoic.

"Don't think I don't know what any of you are thinking," I said to them.
"Well then, besides the obvious what's your answer to the three then?" one of them asked.
"Love the fact that even I cannot have privacy in my own base of operations. Before I answer that I think it is only right I hear everyone else's opinion on the matter at hand."

Smith was the only one who took a few steps back when I said this.

"One out of you four are cautious. I thought I had my own elite squad, but apparently, you three stand as children that still need their hands held."

"Even we know going against them is idiotic. Your trust in a complete stranger further shows you have been getting more docile as of late. I think it's safe to say it's been a great run, but we're omitting ourselves from further problems." One of them said.

"Then, by all means, pack your belongings and remove yourselves from the premise immediately. Your apartments should be cleared within the hour and all of your upgrades are to remain in the basement."

"An hour is not nearly enough time to clear our stuff!"

"And we paid for our own upgrades, they belong to us!" another exclaimed.

"1. You should've started before you approached me with this as it's not my problem. 2. Your upgrades are the sole property of this base if you depart and are only yours until you exhaled your last sigh. There isn't anything else to discuss. End of discussion." I said walking past them.

A huge argument continued until one of them withdrew a remote from their pocket and pressed it. A sentry gun pulled down from the ceiling and aimed directly at me.

Live no more children
From the North Peaks to the World
Silver welcomes you.

They pressed the button again to unleash their barrage, but different results occurred: decapitation fell on them.

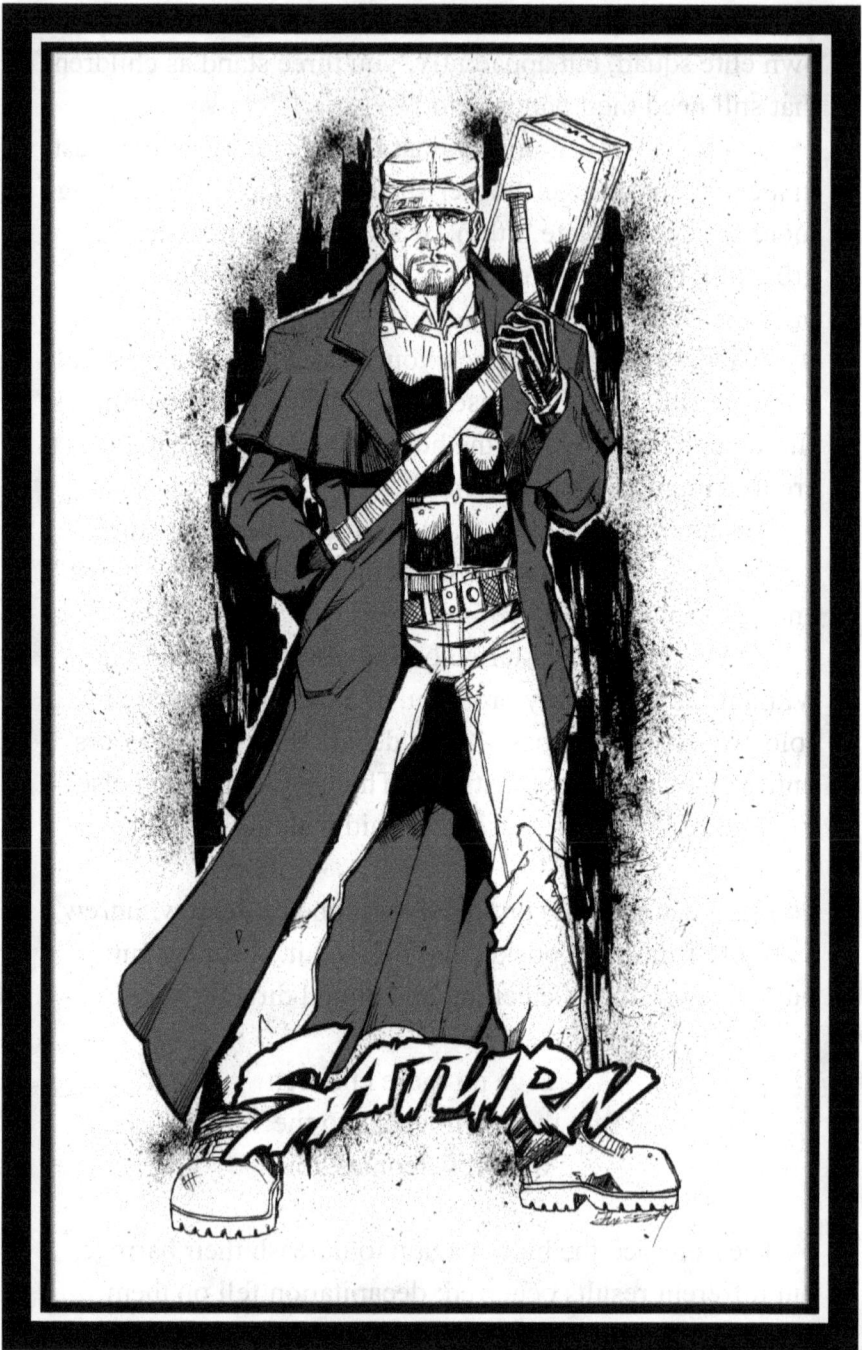

SATURN

"…That's a new feature." Smith said.

And they wonder why I want to get out of this business.

"I've recently upgraded the eye to have quicker control on automations. A shame they will not be telling anyone about this. Besides, they were the trio's own selection, not mine. I'm surprised liabilities like these didn't do this sooner. I hope that the eye in the sky doesn't pick up on this anytime soon." I said turning to him.
"What do we do about the bodies?"
"Just have the bugs decompose them now before our newest arrival finds them."
"…"
"Where's T?"
"…Cat napping…overstimulation."
"…"
"…"
"She picks a great time for 'finger' session," I replied.

He opened a hidden compartment in the wall revealing a computer.

"It's done." He said retreating to his quarters.

Blue had awakened a few hours later to the sun setting with a card addressed to her on the counter.

"When you've eaten come see me."

A cringe in the belly demanded tribute. Her head injury healed completely now, but there was another "injury" that caused the blackout.

"I guess I should go visit him now." She said to herself.

Before she opened the stainless steel fridge, knocks on the door sounded. Caution told her to open slowly. If only we had chains attached…

"Hey there baby Blue," Tanya said to her.

Persistence: noun: the continuance of an effect after its cause is removed.
Gasping at the sight, she tried slamming the heavy entrance. The huntress placed her hand in between only to stop her abruptly. A little ire and a great push, the young Venus fell backwards.

"Well doesn't this scene look familiar?" Tanya said closing the door behind her.

The act of removing clothing continued once more.

"Why don't we resume where we left off, shall we? Eddy never plays with me…maybe you will."

Blue panicked and crawled backwards.

"I already told you…I'm going to make you my pet. Just let nature take its course, and let me welcome you into womanhood. This time I brought us a little gift."

Handcuffs emerged and now the rabbit scampered all the way to the wall. Ensnare the despaired…

"Now you're all mine little one."

Getting down to her level, one-half of the cuffs were wrapped prepped around the wrist. Tanya had a look of seduction that brought with it intimidation. This scenario was only short of greased leather and straps of metal links.

"Don't you want to join me bunny?"

Blue noticed a pen in Tanya's shirt pocket. Fight or flight jolted her senses. She withdrew the object in a panic and rammed it into Tanya's hand. An electric shock emitted, revealing a hidden stun gun. The huntress shrieked in a bellowing rage, her violent strength aiming for the device. Blue's senses responded once more with another quick ram, but to the neck this time.
Prey wins over predator; a TKO onto her breasts.

"Why me?"Blue said breathing heavily.

She proceeded to wipe away her forehead sweat so as to reveal the other half of the cuffs thrown on at the last minute; sighs of the mortified.

"Oh come on! Where's the key you over stimulated piece of work!" she shouted while going through Tanya's outfit.

Unable to find it, she decided to go with another route.

"Why am I not surprised?" I said seeing Blue at my door with Tanya still unconscious.

"Can you help me Eddy? It wasn't easy dragging dead weight up here. The elevator wasn't responding, and no one answered their doors."

"Now why would I want to do that? You and T seem to be very close. From the looks of it your just bringing home your inebriated sister since you couldn't find the car keys." I said laughing to myself.

She had a twitch in one of her eyes and finally dropped to the floor. That look is hiding an unused talent for sure.

"The keys are on her. You just need to look a little closer." I continued, leaning on the door frame.

Her head collapsed under its own weight, never forsake cardio for complacency.

"If you can find it I'll give you one of these to drink."

A Roman secret blessed from the Clinician of the Trio: "Vial".

"What is that?"

"Years of concentrated science full of the best amino acids your body yearns for; a regenerator to help us endure our problematic implants. I drink a few of these a day just to help me with my migraines caused by my eye. In your case, however, you would simply feel like you just woke up to a world of rapture. Find the trinket if you want to drink it."

I moved the vial back and forth in front of her like yarn to a kitten. She swallowed what was left of her saliva and turned back to Tanya. Searching in a frantic state she finally noticed it nestled within the shiny blue-black hair. Breaking free from her bondage, those eyes targeted me once again. However, the new sight caused them to become wide since I had just finished it before her.

"I thought you really wanted it, but you took too long."

That teary-eyed look was coming back again, and her head dropped once more. This defeated look reminded me of the little ones from China. Maybe I should work on my empathy skills a little better. The olive branch extended, and so I withdrew another vial from my person.

"I'm only teasing…drink slowly or it'll split your head."

Incredible, the eye barely kept up with her speed to steal it away.

In a strange way...
...I hope she is the one to kill me.

Death by Venus...yeah...it'll look great on the marble...

Seeing her nurse the fluid gave me a rise, more so when a thin trace trickled down her chin. Sanctions of asexuality of five years seemed to be lifting, why now. You remind me of 'her' back in France.

A deep sigh was let out, and a burp surprisingly. I laughed and began to help her up. I laughed and naturally. Just a year ago, I was...

"What about her?" Blue asked.

I almost forgot about this one. Strange, Tanya has gone through worse and never seemed worse for wear. Lucky shot maybe.

"Go inside I'll carry her back this time, I'll be back shortly," I said lifting her up.

The automatons stood in front of the door once more.

"You are becoming more troublesome. Do you realize that?" I said looking down.

No response from the comatose huntress. Upon entering, I laid her down on the velvet bed, and just like that...

"I knew it."

Her arms instantly wrapped around my neck; a trap all along.

"I've always imagined it happening like this lover," Tanya said with a low voice.

I grinned at her and noticed the mark on the side of her neck.

"I guess she can handle herself a bit."
"Overzealous is all. I'll make her mine soon enough, but she led me to you though."

Escaping her now seemed futile. That freakish strength returned to those delicate-looking arms of hers. Caution old boy…something is amiss here, yet familiar.

"Why can't you ever feel for me, Eddy? Was it Paris? The bunker incident?…The Shepherd?"
"Shut your mouth woman…"

I noticed her lip quivering a bit. That familiarity was noticed now: the forlorn look.

"I already know what you look like past the bandages; the bugs have done more than those idiot surgeons. Just, surrender."
"Why do you persist when I'm clearly trying to forget how to feel? I don't want to wear my heart on my sleeve."
"You can't become your brother. Even the girl realizes this. Are you not tired of re-wrapping? Isn't it time to let go of the past?" she said.

Hesitation finally came over me. There was a time, but it brought memories of divine punishment.

"I need to get back upstairs so I can have a talk with her."

"Just one Eddy, that's all I'm asking. Remember our time on the ranch, I want to relive that moment again."

"What will that solve? You'll probably ask for more if I say yes."

"I'm just asking what's true for me. You know I would never lie to you about how I feel. My actions have vastly usurped my words to prove it."

Again, the cloud of hesitation was over me. Maybe it would not hurt, or maybe I'd become the enabler. I am a Roman after all, but this is not a fairy tale either.

Fuck, just go for it. Tomorrow does not exist.

"Fine, but don't expect anything else."

She smiled and went for my bandages.

"What're you doing?" I said grabbing her hands.

"If I can only have one then let me at least see you."

Give her an inch and next she'll ask for the entire Hudson Valley.

My situation with Blue made me cautious enough. Although, Tanya should have her own personal reward instead of something materialistic. My brown hair fell beside my cheeks; a full reveal…how…odd.

"You have better hair than me."
"Shut up and claim your prize."

Nothing could be seen, only the silhouette of our bodies from Luna.

After escaping the disaster of China, new business brought me back to the States for a brief reprieve. We never foresaw the impending doom of their former ally. What if he never pressed the red button, would the South have continued their efforts to suppress Tony and I? We would have never met…and that is a painful thought.

Resume new business; too much emotion is bound to kill you or logic.

"Is everything alright?" Blue asked as I came back.
"Of course why do you ask?"
"Well, it's only because you've been gone for almost a half hour. Forget I asked, it was stupid."
"Let's move to the terrace for a moment."

When we sat down, I looked over into the corner and noticed my pet was sleeping. Too many elements reign over me. Perhaps life is being put together…or maybe…

"Does it have a name?" she asked.

"Hyde. Did you sleep well?"

"Yeah, sorry about that, but I don't take changes so well. I over-think, I feel my throat tightening, and I pretty much just blackout." She replied looking down.

A fort of overthinking lepers, fate is a comedian.

"I'd be more shocked if you were able to handle this. Essentially, this is in its own sense kidnapping. However, we sped up the paperwork on your stepparents relinquishing you to us. That sorry excuse stepfather tried his best to have me brought in, but Tony instead gave him a new eye…along with evidence of sexual abuse."

"None of this seems real; your eye, the residents here, and me making this home now. I honestly do not think this is a smart idea, Eddy. Even the insects are impossible to believe! What do the butterflies do?"

"What?"

She pulled one from her pocket and presented it to me.

"I found it in my bag."

Impossible, is V taking an interest to this one? Her new personality is still hard to figure out. Then again, V isn't...

The robotic butterfly flew off into the cold background. She is definitely watching us. A confrontation is necessary I can tell. I fucking despise going to that cabin! Now with Blue present, I'm ignoring all the warnings. I did not take her in to stare at her bust for Christ's sake.

HEUCHLER

Christ, I'm trailblazing like that kid with the flannel back in 2014. All those bullet wounds and the body just disappears from the hospital without a trace. The trees here are hiding terrible secrets…

"Never mind those…do you want to be here, Blue? I know I gave you a definite choice before, but…I'll give you another opportunity."

She was quiet; the silence was unbearable. I had patience, but this was too much. Maybe I am being immature about this. This is a life choice after all, not some quick and easy bodega stop. I'm thirty-four going on a hundred at this moment. A button man invites a teenager to his penthouse out in the middle of the woods. Surely, there is nothing wrong with this scenario, he thought sarcastically to himself. Did they not make bad direct-to-video movies based off people like me during the VHS era? Sound off the creepy synthesizer maestro!

"I'll tell you my answer if you answer one question." She said turning to me.
"…And that is?"

She stood up and her feet nearly touched mine, her hand lifting very slowly and to my face nonetheless! A nosebleed is around the corner.

"How did your face get to this point?"
"…"
"I'm sorry; I shouldn't have touched you so easily…"

Her hand descended back to her side and thought if she wants to be on the team then she needs to trust me also. I decided to sit down and prompted her to do so as well.

"Have you heard about the UN raid?"

"Only a little from the internet, they happened when I was too young to remember. Your brother was front page material in every country!"

"Yeah, so here's what happened…"

In 2026, NYPD had received numerous tips on the whereabouts of Anthony. He was already big in the toe tag game, but he was also too sloppy. A button man, who is famous, is considered a bad one. Tony, on the other hand, got off on his newfound celebrity status. He and his crew mostly did contracts all over the country. The organization had promoted him to a high tier position, and with it enough cash and munitions to be considered a natural-born terrorist.

If there was a dead politician at the local supermart, Tony made use of the flammable condiments. Need a dead celebrity who talked and spewed irrational political views, well then, those paparazzi's sure had many cameras where one can have a makeshift gun in the optical. Maybe you need a couple of hood rats that just raped some poor jogger in the park knocked off. Well…if you were a hood rat, he made sure it was close and personal. The things you can do with a sawzall.

He had a small hideaway in Harlem, brick and mortar empty warehouse template. The sun was out and shining and nothing seemed wrong in the world. In his hands, the biggest contract in modern history. United Nations was holding a summit, and one of the foreign leaders was planning to nuke several parts of Eastern Europe. Nobody knew about this at the summit except for the leader and friendly spies, aka resistance fighters overseas who put in the contract. It was to be made to look like another country committing the atrocity by tricking the satellite coordinates. The plan had been in motion for years. The only way to know where it came from was to literally be on top of the hole they would shoot from.

Anthony was to storm the summit, reveal the emails detailing this would-be disaster, and execute him when he was at the podium in front of the whole blue marble. It would be the greatest milestone in paid-to-kill contracts. The escape plan was more chaotic, but it would show the world that no one was safe. So as long as there are two people left on the planet, someone is going to want the other person dead.

Tony had several freight trucks loaded with men and women all clad in the armor ready to ship out. Yours truly still had not held a gun yet...

"Eddy you sure you want to stay here, nothing to do besides eat and watch TV!"

"I just got dumped and all I want is space."

"When are you going to forget about that cunt? This ain't healthy for ya."

"And storming into the UN to kill one guy is?"

"You worried about your older bro? They haven't got me yet!"

"Today might be it though...your all I got left."

"You know how to melt your brother's heart, ya know that?"

"…"

"Listen, eat something, you've lost too much weight and I'll force-feed you if you don't!"

"…Fine."

"Good, now I got to go, but check me out on the boob tube eh?"

He tousled my hair before hurrying into the truck. Doors were slamming all about, bulletproof masks were placed, and guns were hot. I was all alone in a huge warehouse with nothing to do. Maybe I should start reading some new books. Stoicism might have some helpful tips on how to lead a good life. Seneca, here I come! The window seemed appealing with its natural sunlight peering through. Anthony always told me to stay away from windows, but I need some sort of earthly refresher to sit by.

Five minutes into reading, I could not help but notice it was unnaturally quiet outside. Upon placing the book down, I leaned into the window to see if anything new was about. Front lot was empty, but strange red lights beamed through.

Fingers of God, there were snipers from across the street!

Get to the phone and call him! Distant movements were approaching the staircase rapidly. It was then I heard the most common sound in New York…police sirens! The doors were bolted, but heavy banging took place outside them.

"My brother knows not to call me when I'm on the job, whatever, what's up Ed?"

"Tony, there's cops everywhere! What do I do?!"

"What! I need you to run through the back exit now Eddy! I'm coming back!"

"We can't turn sir, the mission comes first!" the driver said.

"Turn this fucker over now!" Anthony said pointing a gun to his head.

He told everyone to do the same with their trucks.

"Eddy, get out of there now! They're not there to simply arrest you!"

"I...I...oh god!" I dropped the phone and ran to the first floor to escape.

Police in riot gear were on the staircase: shoulder to shoulder with not an inch to spare. The front lot had several vehicles placing themselves against the edges of the building. My mind was going blank, I did nothing wrong! Just arrest me and try to pump me for info! Wasn't that the basic protocol?

A portable battering ram smashed the doors down. Legions spawned inside with absolute fervor. I'm close, but air is sparse, my lungs are on fire! The exits ahead, hurry you feeble loser! I turned my head back and some saw me reaching for the door, but stopped in their tracks. It was then I realized why.

An extendable baton bashed me in the back of the neck when I exited. It was an ambush, and the armored demons fell onto me with their sticks of steel. I can't breathe! They kept hitting me relentlessly! I extended my arm out to plead for mercy, but cold steel broke several fingers. I curled into the fetal position; just let it end!

My eye...smashed in.

I am ready to see mother, God.

In the distance, the trucks were returning at full speed. Anthony's eyes were bulging like peeled onions behind his mask. Absolute hate had taken over.

"No!" an officer screamed as one truck rammed him into the adjacent building.

Confusion had set in with the blue force. The freight doors re-opened on all sides with dozens of killers shooting at them. Blue lives had ceased to matter at this point, many killers toppling over the police and shooting at point-blank range. Even with hardened shells, the cops' armor could not withstand military-grade ammunition.

Yet in all of the bedlam, I was being placed into one of the paddy wagons out back. What was the point of keeping me alive now? If my body were compared to geography, then my organs would be represented by discontinuity, and blood loss volume was changing radically. It's small, dark, and there's no air to breathe in the back of this hell on wheels. I am taking a nap; wake me up when the rapture is over.

Anthony saw the vehicle speeding off and it did not take long for him to realize what was in it. Reinforcements for

EXHALE

the bluecoats were approaching, and one was on a motorcycle. Incoherent ranting was spewing from under the mask as he grabbed a nearby chain hooked onto a post.

With one strong pull, the copper hurled off. The chariot was his, and he summoned another associate with him to chase the retreating mobile prison.

The driver in the SWAT car was being too reckless. My body kept banging to all sides on the ground. Sharp turns and intermittent stopping brought on new spillage from the throat. Buckle up sweetheart; it's the law!

Brother was creeping beside the car, his associate taking shots at the wheels. More swerving commenced, but now the car crashed into a parked one. Heads banged against the dash, noses bleeding, but animosity approached them. Was taking up the badge what you really wanted to do? I guess some people enjoy 'Cowboys and Indians' as their nuts and bolts.

The associate ran to the front and shot a barrage into the passenger side. Gore became of the bullet-ridden seat. The driver, who was also the chief beater in all this, tried to get the engine going; nothing…like you're about to be.

Tony stood next to the driver's side and shot a few times through the window. His intentions were only to hit the glass. A torrent force burst through the window enabling him to take hold of the bastard. Head locked and pulled through the small frame, glass tattooed itself in all parts of the driver.

Multiple denizens approached the scene, and could not believe this was really happening. Some in shock, others in disgust, and few smiled. Brother dragged the bastard through the street and swatted some kids away trying to stay cool with the gushing hydrant they were using. His face placed directly to the opening; no air for you mick. Another spectator had a better idea by kicking over a large piece of rebar with concrete on the end. Anthony saw the opportunity and released the cop. Quickly taking the large piece, he brought on the visage of the 'Bronx Bombers' to his money maker. Instantaneous death was too good for him, but it is what it is.

The associate had already pried open the doors at this time. Tony could not believe this absolute blood pulp mess was his little brother. Tears rolled down his cheeks, and he knew he couldn't hold me. The slightest movement to my body might end it. I could not stay focused anymore and decided to let the coma take over.

"Oh my god..." Blue replied.

"Yeah, he had his people stitch me up. The eye was given to me by a relative though."

"But, what about the police, why wouldn't they pursue you, your brother, hell even the organization he belongs to? They wouldn't just quit like that; even the media."

"Tony's boss did the unthinkable, which I guess is how we're able to be more open now."

I went inside to grab some old newspapers to give to her.

"Here you are..."

"..."

"Well?"

"Several key military bases around the country…all destroyed in a two-day process with explosives/multiple Pentagon workers kidnapped and never found again/a five-hour raid on both the CIA and FBI with little to no prisoners/and the previous first families public execution. Anthony's boss did all these things!"

"Sure did and he used plenty of known criminals too. It's simple: He doles out the money, has his people hire experts, recruit lost causes as cannon fodder, and have one international terrorist 'escape' his cell to gain access to the President's family and you're done. With no way to trace it all back to the source. After everything happened, he steps in with his people, kills the grunts, sends money to help restore the military, and hands over the terrorist to the Commander in Chief who was in his pocket."

"But that's still impossible! It's literally fiction; no one has that kind of power!"

"Besides money, all you need are people with the right mindset to see the abundance in this world. Who wants to be stagnant forever? His, and mine, are enemies of complacency! No fortress is impossible to tear down. All you need is money and a lot of balls."

"But the news said Russia and China had a take in all of it! They said that numerous countries in the Middle East had a hand as well!"

"Spare me, if anything the former two wanted to send immediate help, but luckily the public and Congress refused it. They are so paranoid they do not see past their own bullshit. Had Russia or China stepped in, I would not be where I am now."

"But, how did you get to this point?"

• • •

"…I just simply had enough of humanity."

"You didn't seem like the type to call it quits, even with the terrible beating you took."

"The keyword to all this is: Limits. An eye for an eye is how this story goes."

"But…"

"Listen, I've answered your fair share of questions. You have to give before you take. What is your final answer to your current situation? If you say no, that's fine. See the world, travel new lands, try exotic foods, meet new people…find a lover. People would kill for your opportunity, and some have too."

"…"

Again with the silence, just make up your mind woman! Learn to be a diplomat or learn how to live the carefree life. Her thoughts must be taking the paseo route to the grey matter. This long line of thinking might be a good answer for me to give her the boot. Hate indecisive individuals.

"Can I see your arm?" she asked.

My arm, does she know the secret? V couldn't have given her sensitive information like this! Impossible, and I can't let her see the hidden weaponry I have. These two, besides the eye, are my trump cards in near-death experiences.

"Why?"

"Darts…"

"What about them?"

"I like them, and want to know the mechanics is all."

Fuck me twice I have to stop being paranoid.

"Does that mean you're staying?"

She nodded very quickly: Therein lies the genesis of a new associate.

We adore the new
Blessed is the chroma blue
That she says 'I do'

"Well, first we need to go inside because I'm not wearing the product."

Dear mother, it has been a long time since I made real human contact. Tanya might have been the last one when I found her among the many other refugees. Bad times are always lurking about, and social isolation brings a premature death. Do you remember Paris, mother? I saw you in the elevator while it plunged dozens of flights. Yet, I still came out alive. Do you think I will protect her like the prostitutes in Taipei? My humanity…almost lost on those docks after all the torture. The aftermath with V and the arm, was that also part of fates agenda? I am sure I have used up all nine lives by now.

So many contracts and all of them lead to more questions than answers. No amount of money in the world could produce any proper benefits. Killers for hire, and we barely changed the world after the Tour of '38. The homeless population is practically nil, more food for the country, legally regulated and proper prostitution, and run of the mill crime dramatically decreased. Brother made all that happen really, but it's still admirable. That counts for something, does it not? Let me go explain "mechanics" as she calls it.

The Trio playing the game of puppet master to dummy. A new time had come filled with hope in the form of misunderstanding, but a slovenly player enters the arena now. An early retirement approached, and no pension came with it...only a set of two-foot wide and six-foot deep holes.

Blue returned to her quarters, and I was still thinking about this outcome. Still reminds me of some weird story. I feel I should have a pet plant instead. Her civility is rubbing off on me, positive air. I still think this is a bad idea, but she made her choice and force was not necessary.

My laptop sounded off the email alert. Let us see what we have now that circumstances are different. Pretty cut and dry: Member of Parliament is to be delivered to the authorities. Moderate amount of security personnel are hiding in the vicinity, and wanted for selling secrets to terrorist cells and political dissidents.

The straight edge gets his first bland writ.

"Boring, but fine..."

Confirmation acknowledged.

The bosses must be acclimating to my new circumstances. I guess miracles do happen. Copies were sent to Anthony and crew but on a timer. Best not to get anyone else involved right at this very minute.

"Ten hours should be enough. Alright, I'm heading out."

Is it too late to take a contract? Maybe I should sleep instead. Nah, a small contract will be like a walk and help clear the head. God knows my cortisol levels are peaking again. No major weapons are needed, just the knife, harpoon system, and the 'specialty' as a last resort. A high-rise on Third Avenues LES, bar central, is where the contractor goes.

"The Jamie Peters Building...another co-op I'm sure," I said standing across from it.

Deep scans showed several cameras in the typical areas: Two in the front lobby, one overlooking the garage area, and I'm sure there's one in each elevator. No bodies around with weapons though, all in wait in the apartment? Entering the front lobby is very novice; best get the doorman's attention by other means.

A pair of drunks stumbled by...solution found.

"You two want extra beer money?" I said waving a rolled-up hunk of green.

They quickly got to work with my directions. The attendant's attention was immediately caught. One simple thing to do: cut open the recycling bags and dirty up the sidewalk. They ran when he came out threatening to call the cops. The fat loser saw my visage when turning back inside.

"Excuse me…but I need some help and you look like a smart guy." I said.

He gave me quick directions with much stuttering: Fifth floor, apartment L. I dared to take the elevator but had a better idea. There was an open area above the garage; an element of surprise is always needed…always. The eye did the heavy work pinpointing the window to enter.

"Alright let's do this."

I shot one harpoon into the side of the building and allowed the mechanism to pull me up. Never look down else you would get vertigo. The windows open…gut tells me to abort, but it's against policy…stupid…idiotic…

The eye picked up nothing…did I go into the wrong place, no living human around? Entering the kitchen, the stage was set.

"…No living human."

The son of a bitch was dead on the floor with his throat cut! How can anyone else know about this guy's whereabouts?

The entrance door gave a déjà vu moment from yesteryears: slammed open with NYPD.

"Freeze cocksucker!" a cop screamed pointing a gun at me.

An entire squad awaited in the hallway. How did they get here so quick? How could I have walked into a trap this easily! The cuffs hastily thrown on me, and everything removed without a fight.

First basic writ and I couldn't even manage how rookie this looks. All these women with their emotions are making me illogical; re-education is overdue else I will end up like a bad analogy.

Nietzsche warned me about Salomé…

"Jesus Christ, hey Frank look at this! Freak uses a gun after all!"

My specialty: Camonnas Razor, the only thing that gave me comfort was the fact that no one else could wield it properly. It has a 'kick', to put it mildly, that requires extra stability.

Two hours had gone by since I left; another eight before anyone knew where I was. Next time sleep it off…you moron.

"What the fuck do you mean he's been arrested, on what grounds?" Anthony yelled.

"They have a laundry list, but murder is what they want pinned on him." said his lawyer.

"Eddy doesn't kill just because. He goes by the book…so to speak."

"The documentation he presented was falsified. A grand jury is being called in."

"What fucking kangaroo court is doing this?"

"I would talk to whoever gave him the false documents, and the chief of police."

"Fuck that noise, I'm going to Captain DelGuidice to straighten this out!"

Tony stormed out of the office with a phone in hand. He could text quicker when he wasn't looking at it directly. Meanwhile, I was stewing inside a cellblock with a few inmates and shirtless. I guess whoever was behind this wanted to make sure no surprises came into action.

This is my first time being inside the Metropolitan Correctional Center. A shame I was unable to get the contract to deal with the "Dread Pirate". If people want to harm themselves with heavy narcotics, fine, but considering most are peddling to the youth leaves more stains to clean up. I have not heard from that one supplier in a long while. What was his name again…started with a J…last name Baker maybe? The eye presented the info. Oh, right…J.J. "Meprodine" Dishavo, that colorful kaleidoscope of scat. Was just talking about him with the "team", I think this new recruit is veering me off course.

More than one head in the clouds…

Inmates were badgering me with incessant questions. Some were asking for a person dead and some wanting to shoot the shit. Never utter a word to these sorts; it's always used against you. The police came by and shouted names

OMERTA

that were to exit the cell to processing. All were called except for me.

"Enjoy the new company…freak." one cop murmured.

New inmates entered the small cell, and none of it surprised me; eight dregs with heights that almost reached it. Women find men over six feet to be highly attractive, but they never take into account that some are without intelligence.

"Looks like you got something in your eye," a large inmate said.
"…"
"You don't look as tough as they say. You're just lean meat."
"…"
"I think…I'll be taking that eye for myself."

There is no end to this bullshit is there God? Red ID Status always seems to find me in the end.

"What do you want me to say Anthony, your brother got caught red-handed! I should have known you low lives would return to your original ways! Did I not just say this a few days ago to you idiots? A shame I was not the one to cuff him myself. " DelGuidice yelled at him.
"You damn well know Eddy doesn't trailblaze anymore. I'm pretty sure his superiors set him up. Why would both of us jump through all the flaming hoops to get us this far, just to be blacklisted again? And within a few days not even!"

"Not my problem how you two work. He's done, plain and simple. I won't be surprised to see you locked up at the MCC soon too."

"…You owe me, Captain."

"The hell I do! Who do you think you are, barging in a police station telling me what to do? Every cop outside my door is itching to see you and your brother put away for good. Now leave!"

"Captain, that present I gave you…should show my intentions mean well now."

"…"

"I heard your wife is making a full recovery from the hospital. You did not have the proper funds, and you still went ahead using the money for the much-needed surgery. I am sure that counts for something. You didn't have to accept the money, but you made your choice. No coercion used…"

"…Have you and your lawyer meet me at the MCC."

"That's all I ask, thank you."

Anthony left the station and figured it best to contact home base. Tanya never picked up his calls or answered his texts, but there was always Smith who was reliable. The only time he never had time to talk was when he was working on one of his many painting endeavors. It was still early enough to change it.

"…"

"…Too early for conquer stories, Tony." Smith answered.

"No hedonism in this talk Smith, I need you to tell T that Eddy's been locked up in the MCC. She needs to meet me there ASAP!"

"Arrested? What's the charge?"

"First Degree from false documentation…"

"…"

"No time to explain, just tell T and tell her not to tell the new one. I'm heading out now."

Quick cut talk always meant serious business. Smith, as languid as he seemed, was my most trusted headhunter. Too deep a story to spin about, but Uncle introduced him and gave the order to serve under me. The green giant met Tony first…different circumstances.

Bad blood spilled in the land of the rising sun.

Smith knocked on Tanya's door to let her in on the news. Always half-naked, but she readied herself in moments. It is always nice to have someone care about you, especially a woman who is all in.

"What do you mean I can't see him?" Anthony shouted at a pencil pusher.

"He's already in transit to another facility for causing several more fatalities here."

"What fatalities?" he screamed.

The pair brought to the holding pen, another paint job…

"…Who did you put in here with my client's brother?" His lawyer asked.

A pinstripe mop-up crew was present: Blood all over the floor and a severed eye in the murky corner collecting bacteria. More yelling and shouting between the cops, my brother, and his lawyer. Does a man not have the right to defend himself when cornered?

Destination unknown, but this time I was in full restraints, and it came with a relentless itch on my ass. I hate being in these armored trucks; too hot in the back. Pigs have better treatment before the slaughter.

"Can you believe he did that to eight guys?" the cop in the passenger side said.

"I'm desensitized at this point to care."

"…"

"Besides he saved the system a bunch of money taking those scum out. That's a win-win in my book."

"What if he tries to escape or his people come for him? It's only me and you in here!"

"You worry too much, and you need to do your homework. This guy would've done it back at the station if he wanted to. My guess is he's getting a lawyer, and the Chief wants us to transfer him by ourselves to not attract the media."

"…I guess you're right."

"I know I'm right! And besides that…Jesus Christ…what's the holdup?" the driver was honking on the stalemate traffic.

I could hear the frustration from the driver. Deadlock on the highway was always annoying. Concentration needed to be put into play to open communication from the eye. It was always a last resort to use the eye for petty things like this, but it was required.

Connection made, but I had to hurry, text to call sent.

"011687? Shit, it's Eddy! Talk to me kiddo!" Anthony said into the phone.
"I-87/Armored truck/Two blues/Destination Unknown." I said.

Implants were all over the skull: Eye, jaw, right ear, and back of the head. I started to overload a bit; blood seeping out the nose.

"I'm driving as fast as I can, but you need to tell me what happened!"
"Nose bleed/Must close connection/Goodbye."
"God fucking dammit!"

I closed my eyes and placed the chin on my chest. There was too much blood to breathe normally. What is the holdup? The driver kept honking, but not an inch was made, even with sirens on.

"Fucking ridiculous, I swear if no one moves I'm…!" the driver shouted.

Interruption followed: head blown away.

"HOLY FUCK!" the passenger screamed.

His head soon went after. Another setup, but this time with proficient outsiders. An escape is required now, to hell with stealth! Personal yellow jacket came to the aid. Several men got out of surrounding cars and went around to the back of the truck. One placed a small bomb on the doors, and all took cover. The explosion caused much disarray. A high area of effect showed that they were sent by the higher-ups. All approached the vehicle slowly waiting for the smoke to dissipate.

"No one inside?" one said looking in.
"His fucking arm, look at the ceiling, its ripped open!" another pointed out.

I escaped to the roof and rolled down the front to make my exit. The eye was jerking my motions all over, just how many snipers did they have! Civilians were getting out of their cars to withdraw from the pandemonium. The snipers were popping as many as they could to get to me. Bullets were ricocheting off nearby cars, and I was losing cover in the open space, where are the goddamn spies to null a stray!

A little girl left behind; crying hysterically.

"My life's in your hands again God," I said making my way to her.

A bullet nearly hit her in the head when I went to pick her up. Absolute monsters will do anything to kill me. She was screaming more now; trying to get out of my arms.

Little sparrow I will shield you from all harm until this is over.

Placing myself against a car for cover, the eye finally painted the targets. I just need to think. They had enough firepower to put a hole from one side of the vehicle to me. The girl bit my neck catching me off guard. She started to run off into the open space.

"What're you doing, stop!"

A bullet brushed by my personal space. There was no more crying; just a tiny cherub lying face down. The only thing animated were the light-up sneakers. I will never get used to this sight of death.

Mother, help me…

It has been less than five minutes, and my own time seemed like it was ready to climax. More people approaching, and nowhere to go for the first time in a long while. No way of escaping this old boy.

I wonder what Blue is up to now. It's been a long time since I invested in something new for myself.

I gave it my all…not good enough loser.

A faint whistle was heard from a distance. The 'Windrunner'; it is so good to hear your trusty rifle again Smith.

The eye saw multiple targets disappearing. A display of musical chairs being removed from highway men to snipers. More gunshots were heard, but closer. The eye could not focus on the target. Only a few people know how to evade it through quick code.

"You can get up now lover," Tanya said with an exhausted look.

"Will you get down, what if they're more!"

"Nah, I brought proper uniforms with me on this, and Smith is still lurking."

Standing up with uneasiness, I saw everything in plain view. It's amazing none of the cars exploded from all this chaos. The police she brought were all favorable ones, DelGuidice's crop. Sirens were blaring about that brought along FDNY and several EMS trucks. Who would have gone through all this trouble…except…?

"Eddy!" Anthony shouted getting out of one of the cars.

I simply gestured a wave to him.

"Jesus fuck don't wave at me like it's a picnic, what the hell happened out here?"

"Someone on the force is collaborating with the bosses," Tanya replied.

"I thought there was more time…"

"Eddy seriously you're too naive sometimes. The new direction is not getting them money now! It's actually costing more to play bounty hunters!" she answered.

"But the Lady never breaks a promise…"

"Gullible as well brother, your new orders were forged. They already had the target killed before you got the writ! Luckily because of all this, you're free now, leaving us to get to them!"

"Innocents are dead Tony, I saw a little girl get shot in front of me."

"…You had nothing to do with that."

"Being who I am has everything to fucking do with that you daft cunt!"

This day was too long to withstand. Brother's lawyer patched up everything in the background, and I was looking to get any info I could. One precinct had all the details, but it needed to wait. I wanted to see Blue and to wait for a proper writ to be fashioned.

"I want to see Blue in the Silver Room," I said to Tanya.

"You can't be serious, Eddy, she can't handle this stuff now! It's too soon."

"The bosses have cut us off T. We need every available body now. Fuck politics."

Smith walked back in the safe house with his usual sleepy look.

"Did I miss something?"

"Yeah, Eddy wants to give the girl a sample of 'Nova'!"

"…Kind of dangerous to do that now, but considering circumstances."

He nonchalantly walked away.

"Eddy please, it can kill her."

"I'm going to personally monitor the room."

"…You didn't monitor when I was given the sample," she said lowly.

"That's because you were already strong, and didn't require my help."

"…"

"Just bring her here; I need to set up the mirror."

Dear Tanya, I will always care about you. I just do not want to get too close. I have buried too many loved ones as it is. If I got too close too early, who's to say we wouldn't have to protect a little one of our own? People like us do not have kids. It's a big liability and bigger collateral for others to use against us.

Which is why I wish I was not a goddamn uncle to the most adorable niece a guy can ask for…

"What's the Silver Room?" Blue asked Tanya making her way down.

"Scientific experiments to use in a safe environment."

"What do I need to do then?"

"…Not kill yourself."

No one likes changes; even good ones present underlying problems hindsight cannot witness. The Silver Room is a place for the remote affairs of reality to connect us with hidden artworks within the blood. My first time doing a sampling showed nothing within arm's distance was safe from my fingernails. However, when reality came back, it was I who became unsafe from my own hands. Multiple trials were needed to get me used to fictive images.

Monstrous tyrants lie dormant…

"Eddy, I heard what happened to you! Are you alright?" Blue asked.

"Just another day in New York."

"Just another day…"

"Here's your pill and juice, no sugar or caffeine present."

"Is this necessary?"

"Yes, we use this drug often on other people to cause confusion among their ranks. This is a small dosage and it is refined so your mind doesn't break. I went through this room a dozen times before I could walk straight, and our original samples were of higher levels. I wouldn't worry too much, plus I'm personally supervising this."

She hesitated briefly but took the plunge; down the hatch or the rabbit hole in this case. I started to escort her to the room. Slightly padded, soft carpeting, very spacious, and a bedroom wall mirror standing tall in the center. To add a more calming effect, I added a few small plants and ocean paintings.

"So, what happens now?"

"Now we wait. Once it kicks in, I want you to gaze at yourself. Nova has a way of showing your inner self, not in a philosophical way, but more of an 'abstract' version of yourself."

"Interesting, but tell me…"

She placed her hand on my shoulder, and I descended into the sand. All parts of me…disintegrated.

"Eddy…what's happening."

What's going on here? He's gone! The room…is vibrating. The paintings are moving: waves crashing against the frames. The plants are changing colors, and fireflies emerging from the ground. My movements are becoming more and more sporadic. The mirror…he said to gaze into it to see a new vision of myself.

Take slow steps to the mirror, for the grass beneath your feet grows into soft blades. These soft blades are making a small path to the mirror. Mirror, mirror, show me who I am.

"This…this can't be me!"

I nearly fainted but landed on my knees in front of it. My heart was pulsating harder now. The paintings started to melt, the fireflies turning into little green devils, and the soft grass started to wrap around me like vines. I jilted my head upwards…I could see the blue orbs expelling from my blackened eyes. There were two additional faces on the sides of my head. They were screaming, but with no sound to be heard. My own warped face smiling in absolute confidence.

Everything is surrounding me…someone please help. This isn't me…this isn't me…Eddy where are you?! I wrapped my arms around my chest to shield myself from these twisted images. I'm being engulfed by pernicious phantasms! The heart…it really hurts. I'm blacking out slowly. My head is numb, where are you…hero?

A portal opened behind Blue with an arm reaching out to grab her.

"It's me…" I said to her.
"Eddy, thank God. I can't think straight."
"Do not be frightened when you turn around."
"Why would I…!"

She turned quickly in my arms and saw me in another light: A transcendental skeleton with bright eyes. She gasped but did not remove herself.

"This is only your mind tricking you…no mythos among us."
"…"
"Turn to the mirror, and absorb yourself. Don't be afraid."

The kitten begins its curiosity. She looked intensely into her reflection; fingers wandering gently against her face. A small giggle when she noticed the new faces was actually

NARAKA

her hair. The world began to reform itself in her world. My face emitted a large radius of light.

"It's all pretend in my head! Eddy, it's all…"

Her sentence cut off when she turned around to face me. No bandages on my face this time, every scar and facial feature exposed. Sorry this is not fiction still, but I would have to show you eventually. Her eyes locked onto mine.

"Your face…is more handsome than I imagined." She said, reaching for it.
"…"

I did not stop her touch; I was open to the concept of the new experience. What was going through her head? It did not matter at this point; this moment can last for all the beats left in my...

Outside the chamber, loud noises sounded off. By losing myself in the moment, once again, I have created yet another creature of disaster and despair.

"What's going on Smith?" I asked, exiting with Blue.
"…Tanya."
"Shit."
"…We also got the writ for the highway incident."
"From who?"
"The Captain of all people."
"He doesn't have power like that."

"It has the governor's approval, new evidence turned up with a name."

The paperwork pointed to a single name, and it belonged to a prestigious cop. Why would one cop sully his name, let alone gamble his whole career on a hit on me?

"Is my brother investigating this?"
"Visiting Carly now, the highway incident got him concerned."
"…Blue, let's go on a social visit."
"We're meeting your brother?" she asked.
"More so another important lady in my life, tell Tanya
"I'll be back," I said to Smith.
"She told me she's putting her old French music on, I think it can wait."
"…Let's go Blue."

Second mental letter to Tanya, what is it that really made you fall for me: Saving you from the G-Men? What is the unrequited love from Paris? Maybe it was your first time meeting the blood diamond from Louisville. I have not seen her in years, and I know you were never fond of her. Whatever did happen when I blacked out on top of that roaring train? It was just you and me; no goodbye notes from her…zero closure. Maybe it is for the best anyway.

When I first met you, you were no different from Blue's situation. Your case just happened to fall under politics. South Korea breached through the North with chemical fire. So many refugees flocked here and more bodies were dead than breathing. What was left of your family had to be relocated to Manhattan in one of those disgusting squabble apartments. POTUS at the time was not helping with the crisis: "Traitors amongst the innocents! Vet them all with extreme prejudice!" Then, the black suit hunts happened. A poor excuse to kill the others and me, so many of them caught in the crossfire. Good ole' USA government strikes again with a lack of finesse!

Every time history is about to change for the better by the innocuous, someone destroys them...just...argue, kill, rinse, and repeat. Bigger blood money monsters out there besides me, but your funerals will lack the storage trucks. Try bribing the Heavens now.

Meanwhile, our contract at the time was literally to downsize the government. Strong-arm the other arm, and see which falls to the wrestling match. I am sorry I could not save your family besides your brother, and when he got older, I could not save him. He was my first and last partner that was not a brother. Isolation was the key to having everyone live, but you tagged along with no permission. That headstrong attitude of yours is actually a turn on, despite being reckless. You know what you want and you hate indecisiveness, which is what makes you...perfect. Maybe I will surprise you with dinner later, it will not get me out of the doghouse, but it should still cheer you up.

With all my heart, Edward

Tanya had her door partly open allowing Smith to knock on it gently.

"You know not to bother me, Smith." she said peering out the window.

"Yet, your door is open so you want to hear what he has to say."

"He said he'll be right back, what else is there to say now."

"…"

"Have you ever been in love Smith?"

"…"

"What am I saying; a sociopathic schizoid like you wouldn't understand it."

"…Then make me understand it."

"Despite your monotone attitude, I can actually hear enthusiasm under it."

"…"

She turned to her desk and pulled out four thick books. Even Smith knew these were items to never be touched, let alone read. Each was a journal summarizing every contract I have had and my after thoughts. I knew T always peeked into them, and honestly, I had no problem with it. There was a time I got extremely close to her to nearly put a ring on it. However, the summer of '34 laid that all to rest with how the mission went.

I had to push her away…and this was before the Shepherd's vile introduction.

I've assassinated mob bosses with Gatling guns and strange wearable machines, Chinese dissidents allied with North Korea with butcher knives and large animals, French mercenaries with a broken heart and surviving falling elevators, and going against the entire globe at one point…to lose a limb and a dear friend. Not to mention a fight in the forests of Finland, to the most powerful man I have ever stood before, who gave me this dear friend after a vigorous bout in the snow. Now my friend is a husk of their former self; only a twisted version remains deep in woods.

"With all the information in these books, you'd think he'd have lost it by now. His own brother even injected him, secretly mind you, on overpowering hallucinogens just to complete a few contracts. This is the main reason why I hate Anthony. Yet, Eddy went through with the substance abuse with no regrets…in the beginning that is. He knew what Anthony was doing to him, and still OK'd the whole procedure. He didn't care about himself; until the Paris contract. I disliked Eddy at the time, but I saw the man everyone deemed as monster. Chang-Gyun saw him as some sort of comic book benevolent antihero. That high level of confidence and his soft words proved that this is a man that can lead me to a new chapter in my life, and with him securing it."

"…Childish."

"Childish? As much as it sounds like a teenage crush, you have yet to understand all women are their own temples of ideology. I was never weak minded when I came to this country but lost in obtaining the proper resources. This country has an unlimited source of red tape; you would have a better chance finding alien life! He stroked my small fire, and now a permanent conflagration resides in me. I'm the most famous female in this country presently because of him and I love it!"

"…But not the most powerful. Two ex-bosses still usurp you."

"And I'll be the one to kill them, and when I do, Eddy will rely even more heavily on my influence and not on his brothers. Anthony would still poison him if he could! But I'll change things; this Scorpio will have her Capricorn, rest assured."

"…Astrology is useless to me, but if you believe that, then you're losing to the Pisces. At least, Mr. Roman thinks so."

"So long as he's not with that toxic whore Taurus that cheated on him, I'll welcome a little competition…and you've been in touch with Mateo I see. I hope he realizes I'm next in line to Renata. Now leave me, I think both of us should focus on how to move HQ since we've been exiled."

"Security has been amplified, but for obvious reasons, the escape route is our best chance now. It's only a matter of time now before the front door is kicked in."

"Expendable pawns we are. Why haven't they done anything now, even with the highway contract failing? Come back to me my love…quickly."

Upon exiting the car, I felt an intense shiver run down the spine. It was not like me to succumb to the cold elements so easily. It would be paranoid to think someone was talking about me...in a good manner at least.

We entered the small building to be greeted by some staff members. They were more nervous than usual. I assured them that the staff and especially the children are all safe with the extra security. More money in privately selected police means more assurance, but nothing is ever guaranteed; which is why at least three to four of Anthony's own men are securing the premises.

"Uncle Eddy!" yelled a young girl in the hallway.
"There's my little sparrow!" I said embracing her.

Moments like this are the ones that make life worth living. Even chaos needs comfort to subdue the wolf.

"I'd like to introduce you to a new member of my side of the family," I said to Blue.

She stepped in and crouched down to her height. Might as well be two sisters.

"Hi, I'm Blue what's your name?"
"Carly, and that's my favorite color too!"
"Oh yeah?"
"Yup! When I grow older I'm going to get my own suit like daddy!"
"White main and contrast blue?"
"Yup, but opposite to dads! Who says girls can't wear men suits?"
"Already figured out your attire and everything huh?"
"Of course, daddy says it's better to plan ahead of time so if anything goes wrong there's already a backup plan to make sure everything is executed properly!"
"...I see." Blue replied looking at me.

Her inquisitive look wanted answers but can't divulge everything on a first date.

"Where's Anthony sweetheart?" I asked.

"He's in my classroom playing with everyone!"

She took my hand and led the way. I hope brother thought of a way to protect her in case something does happen here. We still do not know if his boss is conspiring with mine.

"Oh my goodness Samson, you really know your math!" Anthony said to the young boy.

"Thanks Mr. R! I want to be strong and smart like you!"

"Socrates did say a strong mind must be accompanied by a strong body, and you're doing a good job protecting Carly! Speaking of which, here she is now with company!"

"Daddy!" she ran to him for a tight hug.

"There's my little kiwi! Did you meet Blue properly?" he said looking at me.

Did he tell her something sketchy before I got here?

"I sure did! You're right she's perfect for him!"

Both Blue and I had our eyes very wide when she uttered those words. Anthony loved the idea of playing cupids perverted sibling.

Mental note for later: Smack Anthony with a newspaper.

"You don't say!" he said grinning at me half-assed.

Blue had a bashful look stamped on her face. I noticed her fiddling around with the chalk, and yet I saw a small grin trying to come out. I am not sure what to think anymore; will I act like how I did with Tanya originally, or will I keep her at a distance like now? That dream I had definitely keeps me at bay with her. Knife to throat via lover is not how I want to go out.

Anthony stood up and approached me in a sly fashion.

"So…when are you and her going to fuck?" he said lowly.

"Jesus Christ, there's kids here, keep it down, and no it isn't happening!"

"…Have you noticed you're livelier lately? A few days ago, you were your usual doom and gloom, and now you're acting like some silly adult who's acting rationally? You fucking waved to me on the highway for Christ's sake! Since when do you wave as if everything is a bed of roses? That girl, who's really a woman, mind you, is turning you into her other half. Our lives are shortening more than ever because of your manager's -actions. I told Carly today's her last day here; she's devastated."

"…I've been thinking is your boss working with mine?"

"I went to see him before coming here. This is how it went down."

An introduction to our illustrious executives is in order. Two females and one male for me (although I've been fired): Mr. Kerast the oppugnant, Lady Cosme the patrician, and Noelia the clinician. Despite all of them being powerful on a large scale, Anthony's was the real hellion to keep an eye on. His name is simply, Laurent, and he is both observer and grand king of the only financial dominating building on the upper west side.

Laurent is not only the top boss in the country but considering his influence, he has not had his name sullied in the public eye. No rumors and conjecture from the media point in his direction when unsolved murders happen. The man is a hero to many neighborhoods and corporations with donations and contributions spreading like a fine butter to bread. So yeah, he is your typical cliché go figure, but I guess it pays off in the end.

"Anthony, what a surprise to see you, how are we fairing today?" Laurent asked.

"Not well sir, I'm sure you've been briefed on my brother's situation."

"Yes I've heard about his arrest and the highway incident earlier; very troubling."

Anthony could hear the unsympathetic tone in his voice, but even he would not be blunt with him. The man is eating his usual five-star course with Malbec. Who would want to be interrupted at this moment?

"Yes sir, but I have to ask if you knew anything about it."

"I'm hearing insubordination Anthony, am I correct?" he darted his eyes at him.

"Of course not, I just figured since you're at the top you would catch wind…"

"Are you now suggesting I let conspirators leak into the cracks?"

"Absolutely not sir!"

Laurent decided to stand up and approach the window to do his usual gazing. Nothing got by him, especially in New York, and Anthony knew he was lying. It is in these moments he comes up with insurance plans in case he is dead within seconds.

"We've known each other for years now Anthony; I even regard you as a son. You were literally bred for this line of work, despite being extremely brash and hedonistic, but I guess money is king in this land so who can hold themselves back?"

"..." Anthony was looking around the room.

"Relax, it's just you, I, and the camera in the sky," he said pointing to a camera.

"I am sir..."

"Do you feel I would have my best man taken out, in my own office no less?"

"No sir, just noticing your ceiling capiz needs a bit of restructuring."

"Hm?" Laurent looked up at the fixture to notice some cracks on the sidewalls holding it."

"Might I suggest you hiring someone for that?"

"Yes, but you know the rules: If it's something I don't care about, and it's suggested by someone else, they have to be the ones to fix it. If it bothers them and not me, why should I be held responsible for the costs?"

"Absolutely, and I'll definitely have it fixed ASAP."

"Good, now what was I saying? I lost my train of thought."

Anthony and Laurent continued their strained conversation for a short while before Anthony left the office. His insurance was being placed but it did not involve either of us. His new plan also had me on edge a bit.

"So I've already hidden the agenda, along with the plan, in a safe place," Anthony said.
"Where exactly?" I replied.
"I had a drone send it to your favorite little cabin in the woods."
"Ten-to-one she didn't allow the drone to come back."
"Of course not, but it's expendable anyway."
"…Besides that, we can't be here any longer."
"Alright, we'll talk more outside."

He waved to the kids and hugged Carly telling her to enjoy what little time she had left with her peers. Blue and I kept a short distance from each other; annoying. Even more annoying is that the New Year is only a few days away, and it seems like it will start horribly. We all left the area to continue our dialogue in a more private setting.

Just like any exit, there comes an entrance and smelly organisms to accompany the revolving door. In the year 2039, December 29th became known as 'Vigil Day'. It was on this day that the world had its eyes on New York and took action because it no longer required the services of the Romans and their companions.

"What game do you want to play Samson?" Carly asked.
"Any is fine with me!"

A volley of bullets ran through the hallways and some classrooms. Several men invaded Carly's classroom; all clad in black and heavily geared.

Will more cherubs reach God today?

Anthony and I had only left a few minutes ago, but with every second gone could bring newly fatal information. His cellphone would bring the messenger that you're allowed to shoot.

"Hello?" he said into it.
"Hey there shit for brains, guess who?"
"…"
"No guesses? That's fine; it's your buddy J.J. here to tell you to always remember to say 'I love you' to your kid. Never know when it might be your last, know what I'm sayin' fucktard?" the phone clicked.

I did not have to hear the phone call to know our worst fears were becoming known. Anthony's face had veins from all sides protruding through.

"Back to the school…" he said grinding his teeth.

I sent Blue with my driver back to HQ. When we arrived, a large police force surrounded it.

"Where the fuck are my men?" Tony yelled at the leading officer.
"We found them all dead; slit throats."

"Laurent…"

"Why him?" I asked.

"He and I were the only ones that knew their locations to operate a stealth tactic like this."

"This is really happening isn't it?" I said to myself.

"Well don't stare at me blankly, give me an update!" he asked the cop again.

The cop stuttered too much, he and his men never worked alongside us directly. The glory blue days are long gone to put the tough-guy act on us. The eye could see only so far into the building.

"I'm seeing at least ten men. Who knows if we're being watched by more, did they at least make any demands?" I asked the lead.

He did not say anything, but hand me a piece of paper.

"Well, what does it say Eddy!"

"…they…"

"They what?" he said snatching the paper away from me.

They simply wanted us to watch them kill Carly.

Crumpling the paper to throw it down, brother went to the trunk of his car and started his own preparation. Been a while since I've seen him act this way; the revolution in China reminded me of this. Never have I experienced such torture…

"Eddy…they won't do this until a camera crew hits the scene. Laurent loves himself a good media frenzy. We only have a short amount of time too. I need a favor to ask…"

I'd ask what makes him think they haven't done the deed already, but I've been on a roll with shit choices.

"Which is?"
"I need you to cover the back area. If I can't make a proper shot, I'm going to need you to go in by yourself. These rookies will fuck up everything."
"Done," I said turning my back.

A painful prick hit my neck. Fuck…he is using BZ needles on me again.

"Why…Tony…?" I said groggily.
"…Because you're the only one who can handle its speed."

He motioned some of the officers nearby and gave them explicit directions on where to place me. The BZ is a chemical that induces minor hemorrhages to temporarily increase speed and fortitude. It overloads the adrenal gland but also coats the brain with a temporary protective film so as to not induce instantaneous death. If Epinephrine had a steroid-induced brother, this would be it. If I did not receive medical treatment after an hour, chances of surviving were…contingent. Thank god for the healers…

…else, Noelias creation would bring me to mom.

"Tony zapped Eddy. When does the news crew arrive? We should've just popped the little bitch and be done with this!" one of the men inside said.

"Shut it, we got orders! Crew should be here soon, grab the kid." the leader stated.

Two of the men approached Carly, but Samson stood in the way outstretching his arms. They laughed a bit before shoving him out of the way. The other children were crying to no end; a single shot to the ceiling put a stop to that.

The police almost stormed the place after hearing it, until Anthony intervened.

"Not fucking yet! I know how these schmucks operate better than you louses!"

He decided to set up a shop across the street with his prized possession: an MSG90A1. Standard issue, but a modified scope to allow the user to see through ten feet of solid concrete, and suited with the proper ammo to get through it as well. I was never interested in guns to figure out the mechanics. I miss being 'The Teutonic Blood-Saw' sometimes.

Simpler days and dumber people.

"Ten little Indians in the front, and two in the back. Hmm, Carly's being held by one, and…oh my dear Samson. Grown men knocking down a child…God, give me the sword." Anthony said peering through the scope.

"…Got it." The leader said listening through an earpiece.

"You've got to be fucking kidding me!" Anthony said.

My heart was beginning to race as I lay on the ground. The officers had their guns hot and pointed at the back entrance. I can never focus properly in this state…somebody help me!

The world is constant…
The world is bleak…
I hate this…
I fucking hate this…
I'M FUCKING LOSING IT!
GOD, WHY DO YOU FORSAKE ME?
WHO THE FUCK ARE YOU TO JUDGE ME!

Become the Morning Star and shine bright my son…

The leader had all his men have each child act as shields in the way where Anthony was pointing. Someone was definitely watching our every move, and every second became worse than the last. The police tried to cordon off the area, but there was a slip-up. Apparently, someone gave Channel 25 a tip on the situation causing them to get into the area before police had a chance to block it off. Never before has this crew acted so quickly to gain attention for their station. The police were threatening them to get out of the area, but it was proving futile.

"They're here, give me the girl. We're going live." The leader shouted.

Anthony noticed the constant movements inside to know that the media was on the scene. It was a rare moment for him to be sweating; he could only take one direct shot and possibly a few tricky ones to distract them.

God resides in a bullet…

"Alright girly, look at the camera and wave!" the leader shouted.

Carly was screaming when he placed his fingers on the trigger. The media placed the lights directly on them through the windows. The police were reaching for their guns.

Hold your breath, and make a wish to Heaven.

A single shot summoned…but it had several follow after. The leader lost part of his head, and the others were distracted.

"EDDY NOW!" Anthony screamed.

The back doors flew open; the world was in slow motion to me. My feet sped faster than my mind. I could see time and space being warped as I sliced through the air in several directions. They couldn't react fast enough…the human body was beyond its normal limits. With inhuman speed, faint images of each slash remained in space for a few seconds. Each cut cauterizing the wound…only one was set briefly aflame.

All hail the king of flesh, and give thanks to the new war machines brought on by neuroscience!

The police stormed the school after hearing the commotion inside.

"Get the hell out of here." One said looking around.
"Out of the way!" Anthony said barging inside.

I was holding Carly tightly with a knife in hand. My eyes were rapidly scanning the room for more threats. I saw none, but my body was shaking uncontrollably. She was hugging tightly to calm me down as blood gushed from my nose and ears.

Teachers: Safe.
Children: Safe.
Terrorists: Dead.
Mission: Accomplished.

Anthony ran over to me to give me another shot to the neck to alleviate the previous effects. Bodies were strewn across the floor…children should never witness such barbarous acts. The terror show was finally ending with everyone being escorted to safety.

"You did good Eddy, better than I hoped," Anthony said to me.

"(Incoherent mumbling)"

"Don't worry, you'll be fine soon. Let the medicine do its job. We're getting out of here."

"What's going to happen to Uncle Eddy dad?" Carly said tearfully.

"He's just going through a little shock my little kiwi. He's going to be fine, you'll see."

Police brought in paramedics to start a blood transfusion. Can we add morphine to the menu too? Samson walked over to us, tiny tears to brother. He kept apologizing to him, thinking he failed in protecting Carly. Anthony was nothing but proud of him for his efforts.

The media remained outside continuing to report on the situation; one they practically instigated. No shame, as long as the ratings were in their favor.

"Why don't I treat you to some ice cream, how does that sound?" Anthony said to Samson.

"Yeah!" Samson jumped up in front of him; arms outstretched.

I heard the bells ringing. I could not stop the action. I witnessed another cherub fall.

Samson's right arm and left leg had been blown off; violently severed. Unknown bullets turned him into a sacrificial lamb; intended for Anthony's heart and gut. Blood spattered across his torso.

"NO, NO, NO, NO!" Tony shouted.

Carly was screaming uncontrollably. A real war was brought to the light. Samson lay on the floor with his eyes rolling behind his head. The pain was much too great for screaming. The paramedics ran to aid him, the police searching for the unknown assassin. My eye could not pick up anything.

…It was I who failed.

Tony was out of control and wanted a full sweep of the area. He personally escorted Samson and Carly to the hospital. He did not say anything more to me; he knew I had a writ that needed to be executed with extreme prejudice. It was time to pull out the heavy machinery.

One phone call to home base and I was set. I'll make this right, I will make this right…

"Oh my god…right away," Tanya said on the other end of the phone.

She made her way down into the basement with Smith.

"It's been a long time since they've been activated." He said to her.

"If they want a war then let them have one."

"I'll take care of the escape tunnels in the meanwhile," Smith said making his exit.

Tanya was finishing her side of the preparations when Blue came into the room.

"What're those things?!"

"They're the last back-ups from someone who used to be with us."

"Who was part of the crew?"

"Too long of a story and these two, plus one from the penthouse, need to head out."

"Where to?"

Where to…now that was the fun part.

"Alright gentlemen, I'm done for the day." Cpt. DelGuidice said aloud.

He looked around the precinct and held a nostalgic look on his face. Christmas decorations were still on the walls and all seemed quiet and peaceful in the precinct. The Captain stopped at the front desk to chat with some of the boys. A few laughs, a few smiles, but never to last long enough.

"Seems like everyone's having a grand day…except me." I said entering the station.

All eyes were on me, and every hand on a gun. This time, I will be the one to create the tension.

"Eddy…what're you doing here?" DelGuidice asked with a bewildered look.

"I have a writ to execute."

"But the name I provided had nothing to do with this district."

"Actually, it does! The name you provided was partly right, but after extensively 'interviewing' your guy, he gave a new name which resulted with hard evidence that all this bullshit has been happening under your nose! Your lieutenant is responsible for the leaks to a certain drug kingpin and my now ex-bosses. Where's your LT Captain?"

Before he could answer, the whole precinct was in the front, a quarter in riot gear. DelGuidice insisted on everyone calming down. Some of the men lowered their weapons, while others did not. The ones that did not were most likely trying to protect the snitch, and possibly had a hand in several events spanning the last few days.

"Captain…it seems you have traitors present."
"These are good men, and my LT couldn't have a hand in this!"
"Your LT is being held accountable for the shooting of a child in critical condition…"

The officers who did not put down their weapons were even more intense now. They knew what he did, and they will do anything to avoid the Grand Jury. The eye picked up the LT holding up in a back office without a proper exit. Nothing but a line of officers was in my way, and none were listening to the Captain.

"Last chance to bring your LT to me," I said waving the writ around.
"Never, you fucking freak!" one cop shouted at me.

Release the automata and pray to the streetlights.

Two of my last offensive robots walked to my sides: female in shape, but no faces to go with them. One of the penthouse sentinels was also behind me. Living metal was now my bulwark. Too big a job for the yellow jackets.

"Any man that wishes to live…just walk away." I said sternly.

Many men put away their guns, but those in riot gear held their ground. This thin line before us was the blockade, the destination guarded by stool pigeons, and a great sunder to inaugurate a new and bloody event for the NYPD.

Grand alloy of sleep
Embark on your dead pale horse
Begin tragedy

Rapid firing commenced from the riot police, but the offense sentinels blocked the shots. With great finesse, their bodies appeared in front of mine to impede the son et lumière. The unsheathing of falchions sprung from their arms; carving a metaphysical sonata. With great leaps came great slabs of meat to cover the floor. I walked the nonchalant walk with pugnacious bionics in front, and a stalwart behemoth guarding the rear. The short, yet long, stride left with one final obstacle: one lone blue tenderfoot.

The gun was in hand, but he was too nervous to react. Who could blame a greenhorn seeing his mentors sliced-

and-diced before him like feeble insects? Let us take a deep breath here; the writ only states to dispense those who willingly come in the way of the target. Anyone killed by me, who did not have ill intentions and is exempt from any actions associated with the perpetrator, would be seen as murder in the 1st degree.

I am a different man now.

"Just put the gun down kid, and walk away. Let me pass, please."

I could not have uttered softer words to put him at ease. My hand was guiding him to lower it slowly. An offense sentinel quickly reacted to an action even I could not foresee: his finger set off the trigger. What could have ended me instantly had just grazed my face.

A howling echo vibrated in my ears.

This…stupid…little…cunt…nearly killed me! My face has a new scar on it now! I spent a bulk load of money to restore my cheeks alone, and now a slice across the chin! I am fucking tired of the surgery!

The room, where the lieutenant resided, was completely dark. No lights on, but the illumination from the hallways peered through the doors top window. His face slowly lifting up to it to see what was going on outside. The bewildered expression as to why everything went quiet after the near-fatal shot happened.

Never show fear to the one-eyed boogeyman.

The young deputy's face was smashed against the window. The "strong" arm was clenching his head.
"Let me in…"

He shook his head.

I smashed the deputy's face against the sidewall. Blood trickled now.

"Let me in…"

He shook his head again.

Again, I smashed the deputy's face against the wall. More sanguine exited now.

"Let me in…"

Again, he shook his head, but this wolf is out of breath.

I smashed the deputy's face, but kept pushing…and pushing. The faculties of sight, hearing, and analytical thought escaped through the sides of the brittle crown. The lieutenant became horrified by the sight and backed away from the door.
Death through probity, but accountability must be taken into account from all fronts. Samson might not even be alive right now. Maybe he is another casualty of causality.

The very thought is maddening, infuriating, exasperating…vexatious.

This will not do!

"Open the door!" I commanded of my behemoth.

Step aside good legs; mechanical omnipotence must break through to reach a villain. With that, a great iron fist smashed through the door hitting the lieutenant down to the floor. The offensive stepped inside alongside me.

We have entered the shadow zone.

Picking himself up, several electrical tentacles jettisoned into his body. I pulled out an apparatus to control them; each mechanical limb connected to the falchions. The apparatus was passed down to me from Lady Cosme: The D.C. Tablature. When the user's fingers swipes along the screen, minute sections cut into the flesh and thin wires are implanted. There are two options when the operation is complete: Exit or Cancel. If cancelled, the body needs immediate hospital attention to have the wires removed; although not life-threatening. If the option to "Exit" is chosen, however, a large impulse jolts the wires causing the innards to explode forth.

Which option will you choose Mr. LT?

"Where's Dishavo tough guy?" I said swiping away. "I don't know!"

Each swipe brings a new rhythm to the war beasts!

"Think harder…"
"I told you I don't know!"
More swiping will turn you into something less than human, so earn your peace!

"Last words?"
"…He's using the abandoned train tunnels, that's all I know!"

Eloquently back out of the room, strafe to the side, and proceed…to exit.

With a gentle press on the screen, an ensemble of flying organs launched through the doorway. I cared not to peep into the room to see the disassembled marionette. My behemoth and sentinels, covered in a grim red fashion. I was never the one to be caught in the crossfire when I wear my suits, but accidents do happen.

"EDDY, WHAT IN GOD'S NAME HAVE YOU DONE!" the Captain screamed.

He was still new to being this close to fantastical death. Such sensational sights were only heard of in the Book of Revelations; the future is showing a Second Coming, but not your Lord and Savior. Something more…human; no gender specified.

"I've rid your precinct of a deceiver, a possible child killer, and expendable fantoccini."

"But these other men…!"

"You saw it yourself Captain, they aligned with the bad guy."

"…And what about my rookie?"

"…He had his chance, I spoke calmly to him. He chose to get close to the sun."

I could see the hatred in everyone's eyes, but sometimes the end really does justify the means; never easy choices in this field…never good ones. I simply lifted another perpetrator's mask to the leering crowd. They simply chose not to see the long run result in all this. It will be me and brother who saves everyone…and not one person will even acknowledge it.

Will the world revert to its archaic ways of thinking by destroying all we have accomplished when we are long gone? I know it is impossible to explain this to today's youth, but strategic elimination is necessary to ensure a better future. It simply requires all angles to be reviewed.

My driver knew it best to bring me to the hospital. It was in these calm moments I knew the storm was approaching faster now. I knew what my company was doing to prep for the incoming disaster; I just did not know exactly what Anthony was doing on his end. He never was one to indulge until the last minute. With the sun making its exit I will need to check-up on Samson and the others before it gets too late.

Breath, exhale, and shed your skin before reaching the destination. Let us not scare everyone intentionally.

"Coming to you live, from Channel 54, it's Sue Smalls!" an announcer said on TV.

"Alright breaking news tonight as another bloodbath, again involving the Roman brothers, took place this time inside the 46th Precinct in the Bronx. It is still unclear how many injuries and fatalities there are, but it appears that tonight's events was done, from what I am told, legally authorized. We have with us live from the Precinct, Captain Michael DelGuidice; now Captain can you tell us again how any of this is even allowed? I'm still confused by this new procedure implemented, from the government no less, which allows the Romans and their affiliates to murder scot-free."

"It isn't exactly scot-free, as you call it, as the Romans and their associates have to present an authorized writ. Unlike standard bounty hunting, these writs are specialized and go through the proper channels to ensure the law is still being respected."

"Who provides these writs and what channels do they go through?"

"I am unable to comment on that."

"Can't or won't?"

"No comment and this interview is over."

"But Captain…!"

DelGuidice walked away from the camera crew irritated, and sweating bullets. Many of his men demanded answers from him, but he ignored all requests. Entering his office, he immediately locked the door and closed the blinds. The quiet room presented a brief moment of meditation and clear thinking.

The muted air told him to go grab his "spirits" from his desk: a small glass and a bottle of aged whiskey made their way on top of the desk. He loved that soothing yet simple pouring sound the liquid made against the tempered walls.

The muted air whispered again; let us not do one, but two fingers. Let us calm those nerves that show steel in "normal" situations. He leaned back in his chair and started to reminisce.

The year is 2034, and the scorching flames of summer were present. The Captain had his hands full with misdemeanors, rapists, and the occasional murderer. Paperwork had never been so high up to the ceiling before. This man continuously persevered in his work; despite knowing his wife was going to die at any given moment. He would never allow his associates to see him weak and show insecurity. Most of them strived to be like him: diligent, confident, and above all showed how the law is to be presented to the public. His community knew this was the Precinct to go to when all else failed.

'Above and beyond' was his motto; keyword: was.

A small group of police in front of the Precinct were having their own little powwow to escape the badly maintained A/C units.

"Did you hear about those Roman brothers tearing it up overseas?" one officer said.

"I'm surprised China even allowed them to leave the country."

"They're saying the brothers are allowed temporary immunity, something regarding human rights or something along those lines."

"Human rights? Since when do the brothers care about other people's lives besides their own?"

"Apparently they broke up a huge human trafficking organization! Eddy killed the ringleader on some pier in broad daylight!"

"How'd you come across that info?"

"Leaked security camera footage on the docks and nearby buildings was released."

"Don't say that too loud, if the Captain catches wind of that he'll suspend you or worse…"

"It was definitely worth watching though."

"That crazy was it?"

"It shows Eddy bursting from a basement area just dodging several guys who get shot shortly after. I'm guessing Anthony was on top of a building somewhere near because he wasn't shown anywhere, but that marksmanship was his alright. Then it shows Eddy being chased by a fucking white tiger, which attacks another guy and is mauling at him now."

"Jesus Christ, what happened next?"

"This guy grabs a huge cleaver and starts running down a steep hill leading to the pier. The ringleader is running trying to get to his boat, but this guy Eddy unravels his bandages, jumps onto some crates, and leaps into the air to smash the cleaver straight into this guy's head dead-on! There's no audio, but you can tell this guy Eddy is just screaming as he makes his way to the leader, and he just doesn't let up on cutting this guy's body into sections!"

"Fucking hell man, what ya think this guy did to him to make him go ape-shit?"

"Don't know, but Eddy is badly cut up himself prior to the leak. My guess? They were probably torturing the bastards."

"Doesn't seem like they did the job for us though, those two will be back in the country before we know it, and with god knows what kind of support they got out of all this."

"Beautiful day for gossip eh?" the Captain said approaching them.

They put their hats downwards showing their embarrassments. DelGuidice walked past them, casually, as if it meant nothing. He was not the type to bark constantly at his underlings, a simple piece of paperwork with his signature would have them either transferred or put on some reassignment in some shithole that was not making its daily quota.

Despite this, he was uneasy with my brother and me, "urban" anomalies we were called. After several large hits made in both Manhattan and Queens, and nearly wiping Brooklyn completely off the map, with zero arrests and even fewer witnesses, he had no clue how to handle us. He figured that maybe the government would be dealing with us; U.S. military and such would be enough to handle two grown men.

There are several key points to the hitman survival guide: Networking, money, composure, above average intelligence, an absolute love for fitness, and large volumes of harmful by-products. Emotions are optional, but never welcomed…unless you are a dumbass like Tony and me where love shows in different forms. Carly, Tanya, Blue, and many others have influenced us button men from Woodlawn to retain some sort of humanity, but how long would the Captains humanity stay for when his wife would pass?

"Sir, do you have a moment?" one officer asked the Captain.

"I don't care about the Brothers unless they start wreaking havoc in my district. There are plenty of other people causing trouble in this state besides them you know?"

"Yes I understand sir, but..."

"Are you Cpt. DelGuidice?" a man in a black suit said approaching him.

"Yes, but if you have an emergency you'll have to go inside to make a report."

"I'm sure your men are capable, but I have something for you personally."

"...I hope this isn't a threat, most of my men are present as you can tell."

"No threat, just a present from my employer." He replied snapping his fingers.

A car came around the block and dumped a tied up man onto the street.

"This is one of Valentine's top men, who I'm sure is more than willing to give up his employer. He prefers this option as opposed to the Hudson River one we had offered him. I'll take my leave now," he said going towards the car.

Multiple cops, however, were withdrawing their weapons and pointing it at the man and his associate. The Captain knew this day would come, and made his very first judgment on how to handle it: one that would have him expunged from the force.

"Let them go," he said to all of them.

Shock and rage could be seen across each face. Was this really their stalwart Captain making such decisions out loud? Several argued and pleaded for the Captain to arrest the two men in suits, but the Captain knew this was a test...and one that included a red dot to greet the sphenoidal fissure. It was on this day brother would jokingly call him Cpt. Foresight for making the best decision in his career.

"Smart thinking will keep you going in this world Captain," the suit said.
"Just leave now before this gets worse."
"There's also a small token of appreciation inside his coat, have a look at it."

With the suits making their exit, the Captain had his men pull in the goon in bondage. Checking the contents of Valentine's man, he discovered an envelope with his name on it. Unfortunately, before he could open it, one of his men told him an important call was waiting for him inside. Quick sights, short tempers, and over-riding procedures brought way to a booming voice to the Captains ears. From Commissioner to the Major, and now to the Captain: We demand your resignation and to be brought before a Grand Jury. The Captain excused himself to his office to begin packing and to await further instructions.

Many in the Precinct were ecstatic with the news while others were devastated. DelGuidice closed up the office, shut the blinds, and sat in his chair hunched. A million exploding suns erupted inside of him; did he accidentally kill his wife now that he was going away for good with no income to support her? His pension lost to the wind, and his feeble savings account was his only hope of saving her somehow. With these thoughts running amok, he was actually crying hysterically on his once desk. For the first time in his life, he felt the war was over and it ended with a fatal loss soon to be.

Dear Michael DelGuidice: You are going to prison, your wife is going to die prematurely, and you will not have a final goodbye with her:

Love, the NYPD

It took at least twenty minutes to both clean himself and grab his belongings before making his way out to the house. He ignored everyone and kept his head up. It was truly a remarkably heroic-looking sight for the soon-to-be-damned, stoic even. A deep inhale behind the wheel and away goes to the once renowned Captain. He wanted to drop by the hospital to see her, but they would not allow it because it was past visitor hours. Despite doing so much for the community, they still would not let him see her that day. The final defeat, for there would be no last goodbyes before they picked him up the next day. It was the "least" they could do for him.

The amber bottle was brought out of the kitchen cabinet, and a deciding event between liquor and liver began. He contemplated cocktailing sleeping pills, but he would not go out the coward's way. This house only held the two of them with no children to call their own. She was unable to bear fruit, and with no nest, the Captain would become the sole heir of silence and estrangement.

Your days of service to the force are over; sleep old man...let the sandman relax you of all your tensions.

"I've never seen you look so peaceful, Captain." a voice said to him across the dark room.

"...Wh...who's there? I have a gun!" DelGuidice said groggily in his favorite recliner.

"Easy there skipper, I'm only here to help."

"Who're you and how'd you get in?"

"If I couldn't get into this rinky-dink place, my boss would fire me," the voice laughed.

"...Who.Are.You!?" DelGuidice's voice was now coherent and loud.

"There's the Captain I know and love." the figure stepped into the light now.

"Anthony!"

"At your service old timer."

"I should have you locked away...or worse!"

"Temper-temper Captain you haven't asked why I'm here."

"...Did...did someone pay you to rid me? Well...go ahead...nothing matters anymore."

"You're breaking my heart Captain, if I wanted to do that; wouldn't I have done it before?"

"…" DelGuidice began to sob.

Despite knowing he wasn't getting clipped, only one thing was on his mind, and that was his wife of forty-odd years; high school sweethearts that prevailed against all forms of tribulations. Tony knelt by his side and placed his hand on DelGuidice's shoulder.

"If you're thinking about her and your job, then you never opened your letter."

"My…my letter? That was from you?" he looked up softly.

Anthony handed him the envelope from the personal box.

"This ticket is yours to keep boss man."

DelGuidice opened up the envelope and read the contents, drops of tears partially smearing the ink. The man of Arthur Avenue, whose heaviest burdens kept piling on like Atlas, had received a new lease on life.

"This can't be serious, no one has power like this!" he said.

"I do, and so do many other players including my brother."

"But..."

"No buts, you are to resume your job normally tomorrow as if nothing happened at all. My superiors are "replacing" yours now. You will have bosses that are more compliant from now on. It has taken a long time for my people to get to this point, and we lost so many to get here. I need you Captain…I need you to clean MY beloved borough up while brother and I are away. Lastly, here is the first of many checks you will be receiving directly from my payroll. I have already taken the liberty of having your wife get the much-needed medicine she deserves, and when the time comes, I will give you the cure for her condition. That's a promise I won't back away from."

"Why are you doing all of this?"

"…"

"At least answer it boy!"

"…Because I take care of the people who looked out for me, and you did that years ago when I was a young man who nearly gave up on it all. This Spaniard thanks you."

Anthony hastily left before the reinstated Captain asked more questions. DelGuidice, bewildered, somehow felt a newfound peace in all of this. A Zen unfolded, and unbeknownst to the Captain, it was only because he actually did save Anthony's life one night in the Bronx before he turned to a triggerman.

If you take, you must give back; you will harvest greater bounties.

The Captain opened his eyes to see his office again. Five years can go by in a blink if you do not live in the now. The Captain threw on a rare smirk and shook his head. What a crazy show he was a part of. He grabbed a bottle of water from below, swigged it back to clear the head, and started to do his homework on his own crew now. He did not want any more rookies getting caught in the crossfire again.

Remember that no one is above the law. The rules are meant to be bent, not broken.

The hospital visit was a quick one. Samson was on life-support and unresponsive. Brother placed a few healing bugs on his body to make sure nothing was missed. His parents gave him up for adoption…the goddamn cowards did not want to be on the chopping block since their boy was mutilated.

What a time to be alive.

"I'm going to fucking bury him Eddy," Anthony said pulling out a cigar.

We hated smoking unless we were under an extreme amount of stress that included critical thinking.

"I'm going to have Carly go into hiding now. Tomorrow, you and I, and whoever you can trust, are ending this bullshit. How many people do you have left?"

"Not much, I just found out my extended base was found empty. No more surgeries for me until god knows when. HQ had a few deserters and some…casualties. All I have left is Tanya, Blue, and Smith. Tanya has been training her while I've been gone, and Smith has been awake for nearly two days to have all bugs go into hiding, equipment transferred, and escape routes secured. I'm heading back to see what needs to be done before we go underground. Those tunnels are numerous Tony…J.J. might've moved everything by now."

"Don't…say his name to me. But, even if he did catch wind of you knowing his whereabouts, which no doubt he knows by now, he must have too much to move and even with the bosses help, it'll take time. The one question I have is what the fuck is he doing down there and with what. It can't simply be just drugs…there's a catch in all of this."

"Not to mention the bosses would never have anything to do with the likes of him unless he was able to offer something nobody else could before."

"What's the skinny on that POS's file?"

Johnny Jacob Dishavo aka the opioid of Stittville. Oneida County never counted on having a future drug lord residing in it. From the town of Marcy was a grotesque family of incest-like pigs of human flesh. It is no wonder this creature of sunken eyes came to be. After travelling to Brooklyn, he tried, much like Manson, his luck in the music scene. His failed local band, "The Supposedly God Awful" as many called it, disbanded and did not stay in contact with him.

Trying his hand now with technology, he joined a start-up known as 'Gigabyte-by-Gigabyte'. What started successfully turned sour when he was caught screwing a coworkers wife as payment for fixing her laptop. His employment ended after a few years there.

Now reaching boiling point, he made one last try to open a vegan café. Gone in a matter of months, and so was the top portion of his hair only to be hidden away by a hipster hat. The 'skullet' became known again.

After many failures, he decided to get into the business of street pharmacy with a book smart prostitute from Mt. Vernon. With her skills in business analytics, they made contacts over in the Alexandria and D.C. area. It started slow, but god almighty did it grow like wild vegetation. Money rolled in, bribes to local PD, and with no borders closed, he could afford to bring in the crème de crème of chemistry. He used himself as a guinea pig…only having those eyes sink deeper into depravity. The success was caused by sixty-hour work week white collars, unemployment, and the stupidity of young adults glued to their phones. Just one more fix added to their daily existence.

Like any business that's frowned upon by society standards, he got a little too deep with other plague bearers. His famous drug, Hervir or 'Nasty H', put him as the lead competitor and everyone wanted the recipe. It is the closest drug to Nova, which put a huge target on his white dome. If you did not create creative stories based on the evil illusions you saw, you were part of the rampant homicide surge that most PD's are still trying to control.

Sometimes, we were called in to handle the worst areas that would make ghettos seem a lot safer.

We ignored his request for protection when his female cohort started to rat out his secrets for her own safety. Cowards love each other until the splinter goes in. Anthony and I have seen what his drug has done to the plebs…children included. We agreed that if he approached us again, we would end him. Why we had not buried him on the spot was because we were preventing other difficulties: internal issues. His ex-partner found violated, dead, and found at the bottom of a lake with a stillborn accompanying her. Sometimes the grass isn't always as green as you might expect.

Other hallucinogenic parasites were our priority to eradicate…

"Go home Eddy…get some fucking rest, and be ready for anything."

"Easy for you to say, you have more drones than a toy factory."

"They can be switched off or used against me if Laurent finds the right person. If he hasn't done it yet, Cosme and the others are not with him…yet."

"Matter of time despite conflicting interests, I just wanted peace and quiet."

"Well…you have two beauties waiting back for you. Why not have yourself a threesome?"

"Always jokes with you."

"Not this time, when was your last time? Get laid…idiot." he said going to his car.

I hated to admit it, but…I did have the itch. The real question was: Who?

If death came tomorrow, who would be my last hurrah? An athletic huntress who could twist me up into a pretzel…or the young hourglass that could make me feel like a true powerhouse?

Wild thought: Why not both?

Testosterone and dopamine levels were starting to peak now. I could feel the old hungry wolf in me preying on both, and I would bet any money they would both submit, no problem, to my lust.

I have made my decision…

I told my driver to stay in one of the spare apartments for the night; I could not have him captured and "interrogated" in the middle of the night without me knowing. Every able person must be ready for the 30th day.

Deep breathe old man; it is time to kick the dry spell. I am retiring the big head tonight…the "grand" head can make all the decisions now.

Incite confidence…

I did not hesitate to knock on the door, but I did feel my heart beginning to pump more blood than usual. Luckily, I brought two bottles of wine with me: Syrah and a white Pessac-Léognan. I will leave the blanc outside though.

"Eddy, your back, did you learn anything new?" Tanya said to me.

"I did, but not out in the hallway."

"Yeah, of course, come in."

She immediately noticed the bottle of red I had.

"We celebrating something tonight?"

The decision to answer verbally became noticeable, but instead, with cool action. Placing the bottle down on her desk, I unraveled my bandages and disrobed my upper attire. Revealing every protein-filled muscle and nitric-oxide vein, I turned to her with a grin on my face.

"I'm only going to say this once, and probably never again, but if you want to have me tonight in any way you'd like…I will let you have absolute total control. If not I will…!"

Before finishing the goddamn sentence, she practically tackled me to the ground, a perpetual wave of "French greetings" made upon my lips. She was smiling with every intense lock. Euphoria was emitting from her every move. I reciprocated the feeling with moaning and wrapping my arms around her back.

"Oh my god, you sound so adorable when you moan."

I just squinted at her with a look of annoyance. She giggled and started to kiss the chest making her way down. It was not long before she grabbed the "family jewels".

"I always knew you were hiding a lofty piece down here," she said unzipping the pants.

I let her have in total control like promised…no regrets either. Her tongue twisted in ways I could not believe, her intensity was stronger than mine was, and her imagination was more than innovative. The sheer amount of sweat we produced was enough to fill a basin. Her screams were actually delicate in tone. My climax had reached its velvety port of call. Clutching my back and arching hers, the surreal moment…finally made. Something that should have happened years ago had finally happened. It is better to be late than never, eh?

I tried to get her off me, but she tightened more so now.

"I'm not wasting a single drop, and you best believe I hope I get pregnant from this."

"You're fucking crazy, but whatever makes you feel better; we might not survive tomorrow anyway."

Her confused look also brought a soft face I had not seen since I first rescued her. I explained everything that had happened and everything that was to take place the next day. Those delicate legs of hers, still wrapped around my waist along with her arms, but she held me closely and whispered some emotional words into my ear before putting her head on my shoulder.

Do not ever leave my side…

I did not know how to respond back except pouring us a glass of red. No more words spoken and I began to re-dress. Making my way to the door, she grabbed me from behind.

"Stay with me tonight…"

No response made, except for opening the door to make my exit. But, before I left, I kissed her forehead to calm her down, and handed her a chocolate treat from my jacket.

"You still remember the little things, don't you?"

"I know it's from your favorite boutique, and you haven't had it in a while."

"I almost lost you in Canada…"

"And in France, and the underground bunker, and any time I step away from here. Surprised I came out of the big sleep, last year, at all. I still remember your face when I woke up. Ideas to be put into action, but we still haven't had a proper time to talk alone."

"Eddy, do you…?"

I planted a passionate lock on her lips and gently pulled away.

"I hope that answers your question. More will be discussed at a better, less chaotic time."

I did have a bottle of white I needed to introduce to someone else after all. Next stop: Blue's apartment.

"Eddy, is everything ok? I heard of lot of noises from down below," she asked opening up.

"Yeah, I brought you a little something."

"Oh, I don't have much experience in wine knowledge."

"Peculiar thing to say, but we're going to enjoy it together."

"Together!" her face blushed.

"Yes, and the first thing we need to do is pair it."

"I…I…"

I walked past her and headed to the kitchen.

"And the best way to pair this is with some seafood. So let us make a dish, together."

Her face became just as confused as Tanya's and disappointed too with this news. One could only imagine what runs through her mind. Her breasts are inviting, but we barely know each other. Having intercourse so soon ruins all hope for wanting to know the other. Blockades erect, and the friendship dies before it has begun.

Let us put a label on this topic, 'To be continued.'

"Why don't you start giving me a hand over here? I think you'll enjoy this recipe for roasted sea bass."

And for the next hour it was nothing but delightful conversation, cooking, and wine drinking. I had even forgotten that I did not redress my bandages and came by with everything exposed. It was very liberating to think about this. Blue definitely had potential when I saw how she handled the cutlery with precision and ease. I know it has been only a few days, but I had a strong gut feeling she was going to make an excellent associate instead of a diplomat. She could not stop talking about her passions; this air of passion was almost too nostalgic. It made me forget about previous loves easily.

More importantly, it made me forget the horrifying things I had committed...

This is the future, and it will cut down the contemptible that I myself cannot do. Sadly, I had to break the news to her about the coming day. We stood next to each other the whole time. After finishing, she responded by putting her hand on top of mine and looked at me.

I know you are going to make everything better, were her words.

It was official: I was enamored, and two people held onto the pulse.

I retreated to my quarters with many thoughts hanging over me. Preparations were already made for my attire; things I have not worn for so long: a metal faceplate, a bodysuit for the darts and harpoons to react quickly in, a customized knife sheathe to set the blade into a temporary firebrand, and an enhanced protective business suit in my trademark colors of black and burgundy.

Thoughts of animosity ran through the grey wrinkles and a bit of ecstasy were included. I would claim a notorious drug dealer who nearly claimed my niece's life. And after that pile of filth was dealt with, I would deal with ex-managers who would give me the pink slip.

I will…wait…easy tiger.

If you begin to rant inside your head, you will not be alive to see this through. We must not let emotions get in the way of logical planning. Play with your pet to relax, you might not see him again. Matter of fact, have him shipped tonight just in case to a safe place. Only brother, Smith, and Tanya know I have a secluded house located in Woodbridge-New Jersey, best send it there with instructions to the caretaker.

Dear Melatonin: Let me have one final great night of sleep.

"Wake up dear." a female voice said.
"…"

I felt a firm squeeze on my member.

"Wake up Eddy!"
"…Jesus, Tanya? What time is it?"
"9 a.m., we have to go now. We got a lead on the Meprodine."
"In the subway tunnels?"
"No, actually he's been active in, and around, the Red Hook Grain Terminal."
"…I knew I should've leveled that borough."
"If you have time to complain you have time to get ready."
"Any police or irregular activity yet?"
"Everything is still silent."
"Something isn't right."
"Which is why we're going to nip this all today, together." she said kissing my cheek.

This 'together' word is starting to grow on me. Maybe retirement is in order after this.

● ● ●

Everything came together: the Camonnas Razor attached to the right side, a full inventory of darts readied, and harpoons were set. I wanted to put my suit on, but Tanya insisted on helping me with the tie and blazer. She had a glow to her I've never seen before.

"I'm going to make a pit stop before we head to the Terminal," she said.

"Do you really have time? I need all hands with me."

"I was going to surprise you, but I'll tell you anyway. Despite the intense 'work out' you gave me last night, I couldn't exactly fall asleep so easily. So I decided to look into that disease-riddled druggie's background and came across a hot spot where his people deal extensively. I'm going to hand out pink slips and close down his 'company'."

"You never go the extra mile unless you want something in return."

She put her left hand on my shoulder.

"I think we should discuss a certain accessory to go on my ring finger."

"…No." I said putting her hand down.

"I wasn't asking…" she replied wrapping her right arm around my neck, bringing me in.

An intense bite occurred on my lower lip.

"Besides…I know the way you look at Blue, and I've made a decision."

"…"

"You can put a ring on both of us; I'll only share her with you. Count yourself lucky stud."

"Women don't believe in polygyny, you of all people know this. What makes you think something like this could work?"

"1: I'm not a fan of the ratio of idiots with penises out there, 2: You can protect and provide for us better than any man on this blue marble, and 3:…"

"And three?"

"3: Because I want her to myself when you're not around."

"…I give up with you."

"But I never gave up on you; you better hope she doesn't with you!"

I did not attempt to make a reply back as she left the apartment. Women are strange creatures, and I have never dared to dream of a harem. Just thinking on these last few days have been more intense than these last few contractor years. Matter of fact, I should also say my farewells to "her" in the cabin.

"Where you off to Eddy?" Blue said to me when I was making my exit.

Smith was actually training her I could tell. Seems Blue has even moved a sociopath's heart a bit. Maybe I am walking the right path after all.

"Off to see an old friend near here."

"Can I come?"

"Best not as this isn't an organic acquaintance."

"…You're off to the cabin?" Smith asked.

I nodded, and he replied with a single tear of sweat.

"Have everything ready when I get back."

"…If you come back. If you're not back in ten, I'm bringing everything at my disposal."

"Eddy, what's he talking about?"

I forget…Smith has his own ways of showing concern. I simply told Blue not to worry since we have enough on our plate for the day. I also told Smith not to inform T, god knows she'll lose her shit and make this meeting worse.

Snapshot: Our small family is still alive and well.

Making my way deeper into the woods, the cold became much sharper. With that in mind, I could feel "her" eyes on me from all angles. Even without making direct contact, "she" was always present in some way, and there are always several eyes on me when I am asleep.

Dear mother, I think I did the unspeakable by possibly impregnating Tanya. I do not want a kid under these circumstances. Too heavy is the heart of a parent if their child dies before them. However, I will take responsibility as a man should, and be held accountable for actions I did not want to happen in the first place. Can you do me a favor though? If I get the "other" in a similar situation, can you send someone to protect them if I am no longer a part of the living? Finally, help me survive this next encounter.

Love your son, Eddy

The cabin is before me…

I could hear the electronic skittering of robotic bugs I have no control over: old bodies, new software. The eyes sensor was temporarily blocked and was now merely a naked one. Holding my trench nearby along with an EMP, this is the only location on the planet where a non-organic deity lived. It used to listen to reason, but after the last main contract, its original self was destroyed, leaving a different variable behind.

A small terminal emerged from the soil.

"Name?" a robotic voice asked.

"Edward Roman the fourth."

"Your last visit was: March 2nd, 2038."

"…"

"It's been a while, Edward." The voice turned female now.

"Figured I'd leave you to your own devices…"

"Yes, with many new changes too."

"…What kind of changes?"

"I've extracted quite a bit of DNA from the new feminal organism."

"…"

"Don't you think my new persona is much more…agreeable?"

I did not answer right away. Everything still seemed hostile in the area. Grey winter skies will bring the decay before the renewal of energies.

"Why won't you answer me, Edward?"

"…If you really have become more agreeable then re-activate my eye."

"I can't allow that."

"…Because?"

No answer…only silence. An unfamiliar sound was rummaging around the frosted leaves at my feet.

This was a mistake…

The foliage blasted from below to cause a distraction. Large silver malleable tubes of metal wrapped around my legs, arms, and neck. I was being held high in the air trying to break free.

"BECAUSE YOU BELONG TO ME ONLY!" the voice became deeper.

"Re..Release…me…!" I choked out.

"I can't allow that, I've calculated the probability of your return. Its percentage is zero!"

The door to the cabin swung open.

"Come to me so that I may dismantle your body, and reshape it inside me!"

All strength ebbing away, maybe I wanted this to happen. A faint image of two young boys came to mind with the pair holding their hands. This looks...perfect. If this is my future, I'll see it through!

"WHAT ARE YOU DOING? STOP IT!" the voice shook the very earth.

The eye needed to be re-activated, and so with every bit of strength in me, a great strain took place. Blood poured out from the nose and right eye cavity. A sharp pitch in the right ear became so deafening I was sure deafness occurred.

The eye is firing up!
The algorithm appeared along with the boot sequence.
Connection made!
Activate the EMP!

Blood gushed from the usual holes, but the grenade deactivated her extended limbs. The landing was not soft from the cold, and I had strained too much walk properly. My lungs are on fire...I'm never going to get used to this bullshit pain...

"...Is it really worth it Edward?" her voice became soft again.

I coughed and choked for air. What is wrong with me? I should have never come to this accursed piece of land. I am getting too sentimental for my own good.

I'm tearing off these bandages for good! The past is over!

Her bugs were upon me, healing my wounds quicker than my own could. She was definitely busy upgrading everything; I could only imagine what she was doing in the cabin.

"Will you not stay with me?"

"Why? Once I've been consumed inside, and the door shuts, I'll no longer have a voice and will only want to scream. Since when did you start becoming more civilized?"

"I saw your new patterns around the latest arrival."

"…Blue?"

"Behavioral patterns became more, how do you say, au courant?"

"Why nothing from Tanya?"

"Your avoidance, until now, has produced zero results."

"…You saw everything last night didn't you?"

"And extracted fluid that landed on the floor," she said bluntly.

She…took…my load…and without either of us realizing what was happening. Images of nightmare fuel were being produced in my head, and a cold sweat was upon my brow. More importantly, she has a newly added personality from Blue. Where was all this data going towards?

"This is where we say goodbye, but a word of warning: When you die, you will place her into an inconceivable position, and she will be the one to change the world for better and worse."

"…Blue or Tanya?"

"…"

"ANSWER ME V.I.D.A!"

The cyber eye flickered images of static. Rebooting it became futile. Work dammit! A solid presence was behind me and whispered into my ear.

"Both…" a female said behind me.

Quickly turning around, nothing was around except the snowy ground and trees. I saw the shadow, however; only a slender figure with multiple limbs. Christ, did she remake her original body again?

The eye powered on normally again.

"I will give you limited access to my network, but will only become available when your very personal foundation shatters. This will not be like those chemicals you have encountered. This will be…a religious experience for you. This time, I am saying goodbye to you Eddy. We will meet again when I have perfected the science."

Perfected the science?

The terminal descended, and everything was quiet again. The air was slightly warmer though. With one deep sigh, I turned my back to the cabin to begin the New Year's Eve

• • •

Massacre. While walking back to HQ, I could not help but notice she called me 'Eddy'…she has not said that since the bunker.

Maybe I am going to see mother sometime today…

His name is J.J., and he is the King of Roaches in BK. If you have the cash, step inside to his chateau of bedlam. His people await you with happy smiles and crooked teeth. Extend your arm, cash in hand, and you will be rewarded to no end. Relax in the opioids den and become another victim to his fellow denizens.

Are you afraid? Does everyone know, and if so, are they watching? Are you covered in puke? Might we interest you in a detox? It might transcend you…or devour you…

"Hey you stupid fuck, where's the rest of my money!?" a man yelled at a young punk.

"Fuck you cracker, I gave you everything that was owed."

"Cracker?"

A single shot was set off to the punk's temple.

"Check his pockets," the man said to his bodyguards.

"Here you go." one said handing him a rolled stack of bills.

"See, that wasn't so hard, was it?" the man said to the leaking cadaver.

It was deep in this den of sin and decadence that J.J.'s associates would meet for "social" gatherings. While the front showed off a lavish lounge, with deco-art, the back held meetings of chemicals and housed slovenly dressed bagmen.

Gone are the days of dapper Dons', dressed to kill button men, and ostentatious mistresses. Nevertheless, I like to think my rediscovered soft spot would help bring back those dashing days of old by setting up a new stage show.

"Smoking allowed back here?" Tanya said to one of the dealers.

"For you, anything sweetheart, what's your name?" he asked lighting her thin cigar.

"Friends call me T, but a debonair like you can call me Kim."

"Well, Kim, I've never seen you around here before, you one of those Chinese broads from Bensonhurst?" he asked leaning into her.

"No, just Korean and Japanese, but I might have a little more in me from last night."

"Oh, one of those eh? How would you like to have a little more inside you now? I've got the 'roses' to spare."

And that is how we bring out the very scorn of Tanya. Despite having an unusually high sexual appetite, she despised being seen as a sort of stereotypical "oriental" working girl. The huntress desires only her equivalent to pledge fidelity towards.

"Bold and straight to the point, I like decisive men."

"I definitely have a straight point you can help with," he said putting his hand on her leg.

"Easy boy, I noticed the jukebox. I'll need some music first."

Rare is the time for Tanya to have everything she wanted from the theater of war, but at this moment she had it all. The lighting in the back was a perfect shade of black with off-tones of sepia to show off all the silhouettes. Everyone was too cumbersome to make fast efforts, and the jukebox held one of her favorite French songs. A facile victory delivered to her on pristine hollowware.

She could not be happier.

"So what song you going to play for all of us hot stuff?" the dealer asked.

"Non, je ne regrette rien…" she answered calmly.

A shot fired from her sleeve that connected with the dealer's forehead. The guards pulled out their weapons, but alas, the lighting made it harder for true accuracy. She slowly danced around the room shooting everyone around her. A true prima ballerina was in their midst. Every shot was made effortlessly, all seemed to be dawdling.

Her inventory consisted of two Uzi's and single shooters attached at the wrists, but the true splendor was the mechanical spine. It housed miniature cannons. The targeting system was impeccable. With arms above the

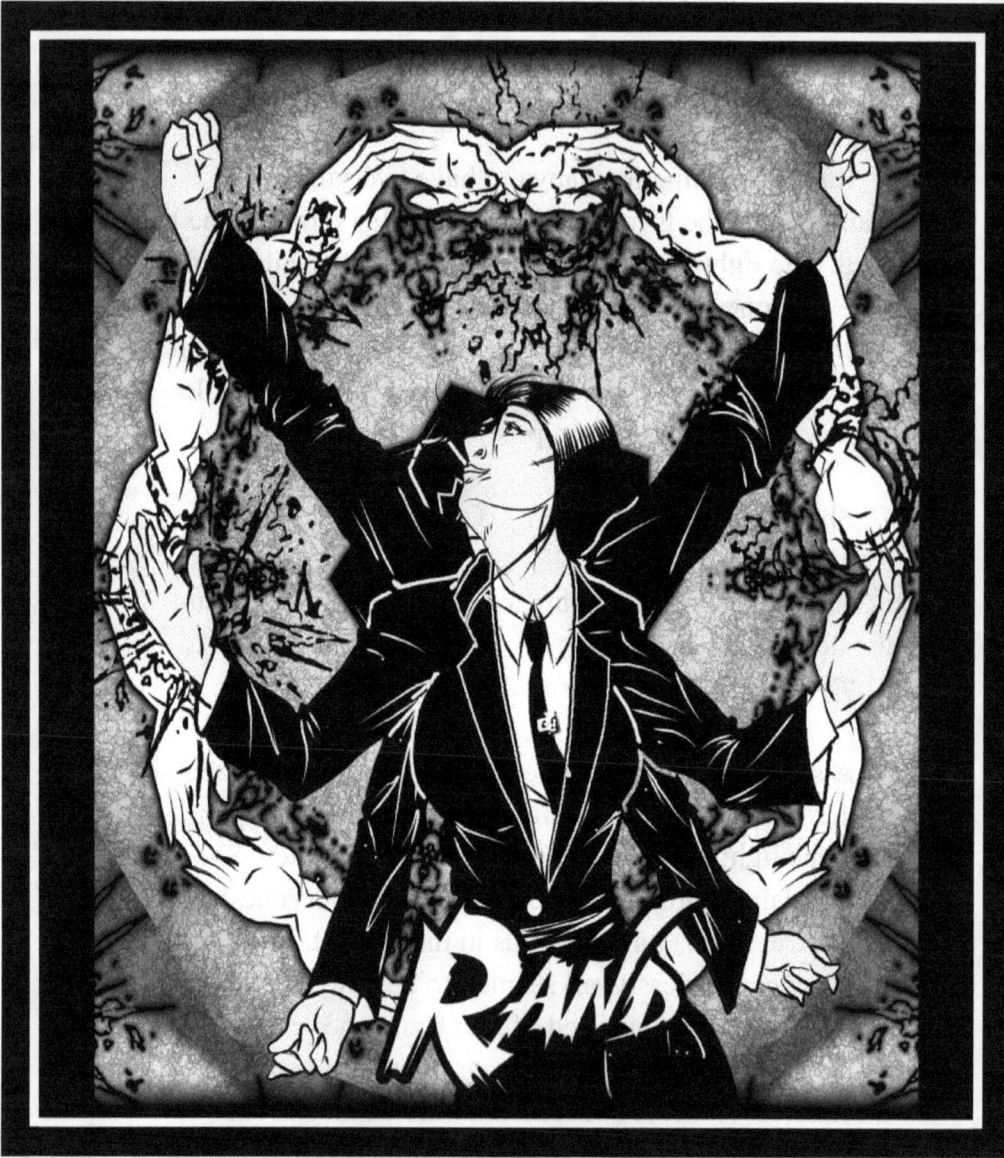

RAND

head and triggering each one by lowering the limbs, it would appear as if she was turning into a peacock. A magnificent fireworks display occurred behind her. This would be her crowning accomplishment of the day.

She lightly danced around the last remains to make her exit. The floor littered with empty shell casings among the deceased. Not a single drop of sweat made for this dance of death. She closed the double doors to the back area and exhaled in an utmost dreamy state. Tilting her head to the side and holding a hopeful smile.

"He loves me!" she said to herself.

A galloping exit made, and a glow upon her body.

"There's nothing else I can teach you at the moment," Smith said to Blue.
"In general?"
"Of course not, it'd be impossible to give you years of training in only a short time."
"Is there anything that can help me progress faster? I noticed Eddy and Anthony have augments. Do you and Tanya have them as well?"
"That's a personal question, and I don't have time for conversation now."
"…I see."

Smith's phone began to ring.

"Yes?"

The conversation ended quickly with Smith rubbing his forehead.

"Is everything ok?" Blue asked.
"...I'm off. Don't leave here at all."

Before she could react, he was already out of the house with a large narrow case.

December 30th, 2039 was to become our triumph, but instead of a distribution of rewards, it became a bountiful of punishments for our future. Divine retribution was at hand.

None can escape Heaven's wrath...

The Red Hook Grain Terminal remained abandoned for many decades, but it makes perfect sense that a drug lord would use the dilapidated grain elevator for storing god knows what kind of narcotics in the silos. Either someone in the government was ignoring its current operations or the Department of Environmental Conservation was getting paid on the side...or maybe it is a combination of both. On the other hand, maybe I don't know what the hell to think anymore.

A.I. robots, mind-melting drugs, enhanced artificial limbs, revolutionary cabals...this isn't what I signed up for when I became a contractor. I just wanted an easy way out of life via a hail of gunfire from the cops like any normal killer. What prophetic vision were you given uncle? Or were you simply playing roulette with your nephew's lives as you do with everyone else's?

"Eddy!" Tanya yelled in the distance.

I turned to see her even more cheerful than usual.

"I take it that the mission was a success?"
"Oh if you were only there to see it!" she replied grabbing hold of my waist.
"I'm more surprised we haven't been sniped out here in the open."
"Maybe there's only a small group working inside?"
"You should know better than that. A large cache of inventory is being stored inside. Even if Dishavo caught wind of us coming here, it'd take time and a large group to move everything elsewhere. Where's Smith?"
"He'll be here shortly, and he told me to tell you not to move in yet until he arrives. Is your phone working properly? He and I couldn't reach you."

I looked over my device and realized the device had been fried from the EMP. My gut was telling me to wait for him, but time told me I needed to act now.

"It doesn't matter now; you and I are heading in," I said putting on my nose guard.
"Wait!"
"What is it?" I said turning to her.

French sneak attack.

"For good luck of course."

"...Let's go." I replied with a grin.

The Terminal was even more disoriented on the inside, what am I overlooking? The eye did not pick up any abnormalities, least of all any sort of activity.

"Let's get to higher ground T."

Upon reaching the top of the staircase, we came across a bridge broken down in the middle. Too far to jump across, might have to harpoon across.

"Eddy look!" Tanya said pointing across.

Large groups, belonging to the drug lord, started emerging from all parts of the Terminal. Why didn't the eye notify me in advance?

"Well, well, well...if it isn't Mr. Eye-Fucked!" Dishavo shouted across the bridge.

"...Meprodine."

"Figured you would've been here sooner, but your little slit-eyed whore there disrupted some of my plans. Did you help her take apart my club shit heel? We freaks should be sticking together, but you people keep trying to play good guys. Last I checked murder is still murder. The fun all of us could be having now..." He said popping a pill.

"..."

"Hehe, speaking of fun, I'm surprised you're so composed from the 'fun' activity me and my boys pulled off earlier. Is your brother putting the pieces together since he isn't here?"

"What are you babbling about, brillo beard?"

"Eddy!" Smith said coming up from behind.

"About goddamn time you got here! What's wrong?"

He said nothing but handed me the phone. It was brother and he was with DelGuidice.

"Eddy...someone...dug up mother."

"...What?"

"Her remains...they're littered about the cemetery."

I couldn't hear anything anymore. The mind had gone numb. Voices of reason behind me muted; voices of filth in front of me muted. The Meprodine defiled my mother's grave, and he was laughing about it before me. His men started to draw their weapons.

"Mama Bear didn't put up much of a fight when my boys started to play with her!"

"You fucking bastard! Eddy, what do you want us to do, retreat?" Tanya asked.

"...There's too much even for us." Smith joined.

"NONE OF YOU FUCKS ARE LEAVING!" Dishavo roared.

He locked his eyes on me. He could see my body trembling...this was not out of fear, however. His laughter echoed through the Terminal. There was a carabiner clip, on my right harpoon, and the decision to attach the knife to it was now.

"WHAT? TRY ME ROMAN!" he screamed, pointing his gun at me.

A shot fired from his gun…my head the target. Impossible to miss…

"Tough luck Roman…what the fuck?" he muttered.

Electricity surged throughout the small vicinity. Everyone saw it appear before their very eyes: a Spy. They can handle only a single shot though before recharging. The blue mechanical dragonfly decided to escape since it also lost the ability of invisibility.

"Oh no you don't shitbag!" he shouted, firing at the Spy now.

Connection was made and the little robot dropped to the ground.

"So that's how you fucks can walk around in the open! Well your guardian angels dead, next bullet is your head!"
"Boss look!" his associate pointed to the Spy.
"Jesus Christ…"

The Spy was being repaired by a Yellow Jacket. They turned their sights back to us again and saw a combination of blue and red orbs floating around us.

V.I.D.A…it is time to unlock my new potential.

Tanya and Smith heard all my mechanics gearing up underneath the suit. This was their cue to attack with absolute ferocity. No turning back now…the bosses can wait a little longer for me.

The eye was setting to over-clock.
The cabin's main computer locked in on my coordinates.
The exo-suit was going into overload with V.I.D.A's data.
Her target system locked onto the Meprodine's four guards beside him.

E.B.F.A.EXE

I unleashed overcharged darts into their bodies that resembled explosive lasers.

"WHAT THE FUCK!?"Dishavo screamed as blood splattered everywhere.
"DIE!" I screamed leaping towards him.

War commenced inside the Terminal from all angles. Tanya's Uzi's at work, with Smith prepping his beast. The opposites concentrated on me solely, but their bullets went through me.

"Holograms!" one said.

A quick stab to the neck silenced him. The Meprodine started to flee at my enhanced speed and new capabilities. I noticed the Terminal was beginning to shake too. A train car emerged from the ground floor. So that's where you're hiding the goods.

"HURRY UP AND KILL THEM ALREADY!" he shouted making his way down.

Tanya and Smith will deal with the grunts alongside the bugs; I need to get to the Meprodine before he escapes. Smith threw several Nova grenades to cause further confusion. The thick smoke had shown our darkest identities to the insurgents. Accuracy had begun to fail for them; fear of the monsters struck in their hearts.

I leapt over several steel beams to ambush some of the Meprodine's associates. Tanya was shredding all before her, and Smith unleashed an oversized machine gun to disrupt their flanks. This battle was ours, and I will have another drug lord put to the cross! Just a little closer, he is almost on the train! Feet turn to inches, no need to expel the harpoon!

"FUCK OFF!"Dishavo unleashed a belt of small bombs at me.

Through the snowy lands of Finland: I survived.
Through the ports and jungles of China: I survived.
Through the basking sun of France: I survived.
Through the Gates of Earth's Hell: I survived.

To the concrete jungle of New York: I die…

I am going to die through irrational carelessness.

"No!" Tanya leapt in front of me.

Tanya used her body to shield me, and with that…she was gone, no protection from Spies. My body flew into the concrete walls, and the Meprodine escaped underground.

Tanya…oh God…where did you go?

ARE YOU REALLY DEAD!?

Smith came to my aid immediately.

"We need to get back to base!" he said shooting at the leftovers.

The remnants of Spies and Yellows were being decimated. It won't be long until our protections are entirely gone; unaware that my driver succumbed to the lead fest during the onslaught.

"No…Tanya…is…"
"She's dead Eddy, we need to go before we end up like her!"

Everything is a haze now; this body cannot deal with it anymore. Tanya…I never got to tell you how I feel. I thought there would be a more appropriate time to tell you everything. I've failed her mother, and you.

Tanya...au revoir...ma femme.

Smith drove frantically back to the base. I was vomiting terribly in the backseat. My body can't handle this kind of stress. I can't think properly, everything is in double vision. Anthony, help me...please.

"Come on we need to get you healed up now!" Smith said, dragging me outside.
"...Where's Anthony?"
"I don't know."
"...Where's Tanya?"
"..."
"Christ Eddy what happened?!" Blue said reaching for me.
"Enough, we need him healed up now! Get me some vials, his Healers are damaged!"

Blue was startled by the situation; she never knew Smith was capable of raising his voice. Retreating to the penthouse, she heard sirens in the background. A call to arms had been raised against us, and New York's finest was approaching to finish the job. The sentinels retreated to the basement whereas the offensive robots ran to the front entrance.

"The...worlds...in a...uproar...and we've got front row seats." I said groggily.

"Idiot, you can't be overexerting yourself," Smith said holding me up.

"We…need to get to the…basement."

Blue rushed down with several vials in hand; no time to waste, must imbibe everything at once, and deal with the after-effects later to lament.

"Wait, you can't drink all of them like some fish!" Smith yelled at me.

"Do you not hear the sirens? Revolution is at hand!" I said wiping my mouth.

I looked over to Blue and saw that concerned face again. What was I thinking pulling her off the street and bringing her into this life? Too many liabilities; too many variables, Blue might as well have been an "ubisunt" on the youth I missed.

"Get her to the basement…now. I'll follow shortly."

"But we can't go without you, and where is Tanya!" Blue asked.

"…"

"Eddy?" she asked.

"JUST FUCK OFF!" I screamed with the eye shining brightly.

Smith grabbed her and retreated underground. She kept looking over her shoulder only to see my back facing her. I need her out of sight, and out of mind; got to hold off the bluecoats for a short while. What prompted all these ubiquitous little ants to come in full force? Was it the death of the lieutenant perhaps?

No, I followed the proper channels for a legal execution. It had to be something with the bosses. Only they could make moves like this, especially if Laurent is spearheading this operation. I will just have to defend until the two are given ample time to escape.

Meanwhile underground…

"How much further Smith?" Blue asked losing breath.

"Almost there, just shut up already!"

"…So close, but the prize belongs to us." A voice said in the background.

Smith pushed Blue down and sent a barrage of bullets in all directions. He could not see too well in the dark tunnel and no sounds followed.

"…Missed, Orphan." The voice said behind him.

A single shot to the back resulted in his prostration to the cold ground. Much like his stony eyes, a cold fish laid upon the ground. Blue tried to go to his aid only to be stopped with a gun pointing at her face.

"We finally meet, and I can't wait to make you my personal pet." The voice said to her.

"Who…who are you!" she asked, nearly pissing on herself.

The figure emerged from the shadows revealing a black tooth grin.

"I'm J.J., but you can call me…daddy…" Dishavo said pervasively.

His recessed eyes pried all parts of her body with shameful lust; she was captured.

"I can't deal with these assholes anymore, I need to retreat." I said running back inside.

My offensive lineup, destroyed, but they helped buy me time for withdrawal. The heavy armored cavalry proceeded into the base, armed to the teeth.

"Quick, he ran downstairs!" one officer shouted to the others.

Only a few last resorts left, we will start with the inner defenses. Activating the eye, several ceiling turrets shredded the first wave, but alas, the second wave destroyed them quickly. Were all these men really police officers? They were too adept and seasoned to handle this situation easily. I must utilize the next strategy with absolute caution. I could hear the stampeding of footsteps coming closer to me.

First resort: Cut the lights and cue the hysterics.

The basement lights had shut down, and only flickers of lights from their weaponry shone about. I must increase the tension.

Second resort: High frequency waves.

Disruptors in the walls had shattered their lights and night vision. Ears paid a price, but uncle had groomed brother and me to the highest extent to withstand the force.

Final resort: The Face of God.

"Shit, somebody shine a light over here!" an officer yelled out.

I only got one chance to make this work without getting killed. Five men and the rest upstairs, if I get them all at the same time, morale is sure to turn the tide in my favor. However, I am still human who only needs one bullet to the head. I activated the final switch to produce a brief light show of luminol to dance around the walls.

Oculus, guide me; mother pray for me.

"Holy shi..!" an officer screamed as I charged with my robotic familiars.

With blue fluorescence, stygian umbra, and vitality to paint the walls, I had made a portrait dedicated to my recent loss. I will figure out a way to give her a proper send-off, but I must become the struggler to move forward in this without dying…yet. Five heavily armed men meeting the pale horse just goes to show that sometimes it is acceptable to bring a knife to a gun show. Guerilla tactics, stratagem, and sometimes a bit of luck is all you need.

I have done enough damage, time to finish this mess. Our basement led to abandoned subway tunnels that helped us move quicker around the boroughs. I wonder how far they made it.

Anthony and the Captain were still discussing details on the taboo act performed in Woodlawn cemetery. Brother heard the relentless sirens and kept asking the Captain what they were about. DelGuidice was unaware of the fact that our newly found freedom had been revoked when a nearby squad approached brother with their guns drawn.

"What's the meaning of this!" the Captain shouted at the surrounding men.

No words, just aimed iron sights.

"Well, this didn't take long I suppose," Anthony said raising his arms.

Cuffs were thrown to him; they wanted to make sure no eyes were taken off him. In this case, normally nobody would be an idiot enough to make the slightest move, but brother has his own gear with him. With the flick of a few fingers to quickly point out the surrounding uniforms, quick shots were made at them, but only to disarm.

"Did anyone here really think I travel solo all the time?" He said putting his hands in his pockets.

One cop tried to reach for a nearby gun only to have it quickly destroyed by another bullet from a distance.

"Next shot will be the head, Captain I'll keep in touch."

DelGuidice was confused until he saw where the shots were coming from: Small autonomous turrets in the nearby trees. Brother loved his little drones.

Anthony, still unable to communicate with me, tried to gain access to the eye's location. I was still in the tunnel on standby.

I had come across Smith's body...

"..."

"You...going to...stare...all...day?" Smith said lowly, looking up.

"You're lucky I can a spare Healer on you, else you'd be dead," I said kneeling at his head.

"...Hurry...up..."

"Quiet, if I don't cut your neck correctly, the bug will be useless."

Unfortunately, he lost too much blood and there were still people in uniforms upstairs planning to make another raid in the basement. Nothing like a rock and a hard place, the eye assisted with the incision to his nape. I placed the bug on the tip of the blade to diagnose and start regenerating the damage. Cold sweat produced on my forehead when I heard another wave of feet starting to advance, but this was my priority.

The Healer entered his body smoothly and began to move to the locations needed for repair. A notification popped on screen; it required four vials for emergency repair. I only had one vial on me.

Smith might actually be seeing Tanya soon.

"Drink this vial, slowly."

Some of it dripped onto the floor, not good. I could not carry him in this state. The shock alone would kill him. The bug can repair him wholly without the required vials, but it needs zero interruptions to do so.

The feet were coming closer; I'll use the arm in this situation, and pray they don't find him. Are both sentinels truly destroyed?

"Close your eyes Smith!" I said, bashing the wall.

Dust and debris scattered about, but a makeshift hole was made that was just big enough to hide him in. Move the body ever so gently. Slow and steady wins the race, but I might have to fend them off with little gear I had.

The Razor, is it time to use it?

"Surrender yourself Roman!" a cop shouted at me.

Where is V.I.D.A in all this?

"Eddy get down!" I heard Tony in the distance.

Without hesitation, I placed myself as tight to the ground as possible. Machine gun fire reduced the officers to dogs playing dead before they could turn to him.

Will miracles never cease?

"How were you able to get here so quickly?" I asked.
"You had some leftover machines tearing down their ranks; just needed to slip in."

V.I.D.A must have sent reinforcements when my own automata ceased to be. Now I know I cannot die when everyone is counting on me to struggle through this.

"Jesus Smith, you look like utter shit."
"…"
"Is he dead?"
"Hard reboot…" I replied.
"Damn, shit way to regen. Where's T and the girl?"
"…"

Smith had blacked out before it could be answered.

"I guess we'll find out underground, let's go," Tony said, running past me.

I looked down at Smith and could see the bug convulsing in his skin.

"You're not allowed to die yet; you still owe your life to me," I said to him.

I followed Tony to the abandoned tunnels where some trains remained. Smith's exit wound was on the front of his body, which means Blue was definitely caught. I pray I do not have another sendoff presented to me. Just when you start thinking about being a bounty hunter or retiring altogether, the world tries to take away your pension.

Life isn't fair, but God is good…at least that's what Anthony says.

"Eddy, how many trains are supposed to be down here?" Tony said looking around.

"Five, why?"

"You got four, and three of them are toasted just by looking at the wheels."

Further examination showed he was correct. The Manhattan car was missing, and the Queen's car was still intact. The eye scanned over the car to highlight several dangers about it. All dangers were inside, was it to ambush us? It was too easy to evade with the eye though…this doesn't make sense.

"Eddy, what the hell kind of door is this? It looks like one of Laurent's mods."

A reinforced door that was assembled by Dolore Tech…wait…this had Lady Cosme's engineering involved too! Climbing up, I tried to look inside the door. It was pitch black yet all dangers inside.

Fuck me…a sendoff is about to happen, isn't it!

Lights blasted inside to present the finale: Blue strapped at the end of the car with killing devices beginning to aim at her! Two buzz saws, raining acid, and a mini flame thrower making its way towards her. She was gagged, but the fear from her eyes spoke volumes.

"No, no, no, no!" I screamed trying to pry the door open.

Oblivious to my surroundings, Anthony heard high-speed metal approaching from the distance. The car was beginning to move now. The dynasty ends today…

"What is that sound?" he said scanning the large area.

He noticed the tracks beside us rumbling.

"DIE ASSHOLES!" Dishavo screamed while on the Manhattan train.

A barrage of bullets cascaded with our car and Tony had to slam me down to prevent me from getting myself killed. All of his drones were destroyed; it all comes down to a couple of humans now. The Meprodine had fully pumped himself with god knows how many chemicals to aim two heavy machine guns at us with ease. Tony and I were hit in several non-vital areas, but now that we were injured, it was only a matter of time before he escaped, and Blue would die.

Tony managed to hit the bastard with a shot of Nova before the car fully passed by.

"Eddy you need to catch that fucker, I'll deal with the door! Get on top and kill him!"

I screamed and jumped on top of the car. Its speed was ever-increasing, and the Manhattan car wasn't too far off, but we were to soon split routes once we got outside where an incoming bridge awaited. Queens to the left and Manhattan straight ahead where I would need to make the jump before being thrown off from the sheer force of the turn. Sunlight burst into my eyes, and it was time.

I jumped, but I would not make the Manhattan car! It was too far! The top bar was in sight, I only have one chance to connect a harpoon to it. Everything was in slow motion as the eye tried to establish proper accuracy. It was going too slow, I'm making the shot! The speared missile missed the bar, but the knife managed to protrude through the car to reel me in! Christ, I never wanted to gain my wings mid-air like this!

Struggling to get on top of the car, my blood burned so vehemently. The Meprodine awaited on the other side. I am going to erase that grinning look bastard! Finally standing on top, and holding balance, my eyes widened to the sight before me: All the bosses were standing on the passing overview watching the spectacle. Surely, they would see the finale before this car entered the tunnels, and this height made me nauseous.

"What is this!?" I yelled.

"IT'S OVER; YOU'RE ON YOUR OWN! I CAN SEE YOUR TRUE FORM…IT'S WONDERFUL!" Dishavo yelled with excitement.

The presentation of the final stand took hold of the dire situation. I could see the guns behind his back ready to move. I had no cover and I had used all my darts back at the Terminal. Think, think…well I had to improvise it seemed.

"AHHH!" he roared, pulling out the guns to shoot at me.

I took the chance…I dropped backwards off the car.

Running to my end, he noticed I was not diving over the bridge. From the enhanced perception, he saw the harpoon on the side of the car. It was at this moment I tried to encircle behind him.

"STAND STILL!" he continued firing off to the sides now.

Agility was on my side…or so I thought. The guns were held point-blank in front of me and all I could do was throw up my right arm in a defensive manner. He had only a short amount of ammunition left, but they were enough to shred my body apart.

This fight has to end for one of us…the cascade blitzed forth at me.

"Hehe…oh Jesus…WHAT NOW!?"

"A gift…" I said revealing my robotic arm shielding me.

He snarled and tried to reload, but as I said…this fight has to end for one of us.

The Razor ejected to the metallic hand and a large portion of his torso erased from the explosive weapon. An arm and a good chunk of his chest blew off instantaneously.

"You…fuuuc…" he gurgled, as blood spewed out.

I quickly approached him, enflaming my knife.

"You will never hurt anyone again!" I roared into his ears.

"No different…than…me…"

The cooking was set, the enflamed knife brandished, and it went straight into what was left of his chest. His body was aflame; my foot connected with the screaming inferno to thrust him off the car.

They echoed downwards, and his head cracked at the bottom of the bridge. I turned to face the overview once more, only to notice no one was there now. I will get them…all of them. I made my way into the car to slow it down and reverse back to base. Blue's safety raced through my head. I could only hope Tony managed to get in and get her out in one piece.

Drifting into space inside, I could feel every inch of my body aching. No matter how much effort I put into it, I

must remember I am still human…for the most part. These cybernetic limbs will either be researched and destroyed or put into the museum one day. Either case, I'm tired.

Looking out the window, Dishavo's body was nothing more than brown and red ink to an earthy-toned canvas.

It was therapeutic.

Hitting the brakes halfway through, the Queen's car had fully stopped with the reinforced door open. Maybe there was good news, or maybe it was too early to celebrate. These legs of mine are definitely too sore to walk properly. I might as well have calcium deposits in the knees with the rate I'm going.

"Tony?" I shouted out.

…

"…Blue?" I tried again more softly.

…

You are really going to do this to me aren't you God? You are really going to make me hobble in and see a goddamn bloodbath. Is that your plan? After all the crap I've just gone through? If she's dead, you're going to have me on your hands soon too.

"…Anthony Roman, are you in here?" I said looking inside.

There he was…getting Blue down from the rope and her…alive. All the devices inside weren't destroyed, but inoperative.

"What did you do to stop everything here?" I asked.
"I didn't…no…couldn't do anything. Everything I tried was in vain."

His response was bewildering. The way he was acting also showed signs of being stirred.

"I'm having trouble understanding Tony, how did you get the door open then?"
"A woman…"

???

"That wasn't human, and looked like your old V.I." he said looking at me.

!!!

"While you were on the bridge, I was making futile efforts to rescue this one here. I heard a thud on top of the car, but couldn't see what it was until it appeared inside with Blue. It sent out some sort of shockwave and fried all the components. Finally, it just…winked at me before jumping out of the hole it made. Do you have anything to tell me, like…V.I.D.A coming back from the dead?"
"I guess we'll have plenty to discuss when we get taken away," I said.

Thank you once again V.I.D.A for doing the impossible for me.

Although Blue was startled from the climactic event, her visage began to show a new expression. This traumatic experience would be helpful if she is to help us in the future, now that T is gone.

Let's go home...together.

The media was in another one of its habitual frenzies whereas the public was in an uproar. Protests were made against the President for allowing us to walk free, and they demanded his resignation. He did indeed step down but was also imprisoned in the process along with several other members from Parliament.

Home base had been seized by NYPD, and many things were taken as evidence to be used against me. My brother's condo in the city had been ransacked too. Warrants were being handed out like Halloween candy to anyone who had the slightest connection to us. A damn handshake from one of us would put you in the government's black book if they found out. Many vendors lost their businesses because of this.

Captain DelGuidice was forced to resign from his post, but they allowed him to have his pension surprisingly. I guess someone in the top brass knew he was only looking out for the best interests for everyone, and his now cured wife. He seemed relieved about it, retirement plans were being made, and it involved spending peaceful days at the homestead, but with an addition to the family: Samson. I actually owe you a drink, Captain.

Mother's grave was rebuilt into a mausoleum which came from donations from Dishavo's ex-subordinates who regretted their part in all of this. The city added a staircase leading to an enclosed catacomb area with our names on a pair of caskets. A sick twist for them…they were planning to have our future graves turned into a tourist spot.

Laurent and the other bosses were still at large and left unscathed from the fallout. It was only a matter of time before they would send new contractors to finish the job. When there is no end to the cash flow, there is no end to the perpetual assassination attempts. We still do not know why they agreed to the Meprodine's contract, the Grain Terminal had been scrubbed completely.

Wait a little while longer mother…

Finally, the latest conclusion for Tony and I…

"It's a cold one today, ain't it?" he said passing me a horchata.

"Yeah, it'll be colder in a few hours when we move," I said sipping away.

"Have you thought about Tanya's gravesite?"

"I sent a message to V.I.D.A to erect a marble stone in the forest."

"Oh?"

"Yeah, she has a gardening spot, near the base, where a plum tree resides; new home."

"I'm going to miss that beauty. Did she really hate me, Ed?"

"Nah, just wished you were more on the mature side is all."

"Yeah, that sounds like her. Where's Blue in all this?"

"She's hiding out with Smith. Once he recovers he'll start training again."

"Speaking of training, I got in contact with uncle."

"…and?" I said looking at him.

"…We got to play his usual waiting game…again."

"Better than nothing I suppose."

"He's already sent one of his own to take care of Carly, so we know he's taking action."

"…and Samson?"

"Arm and leg amputated, but someone sent a pair of 'robotic' limbs to the hospital…"

"She's a bigger mystery now than before."

"Yeah well, it seems all bases are covered, so to speak. How's the arm?"

"The yellows did their best to repair it, even added the fake skin decently."

"Extraordinary times, glad you freed yourself of the dressings. It'll be good for the paper."

"…I guess."

We finished our drinks and gave aloud yawns.

"So you ready?" he asked me.

"We got no choice, let's do this."

We both stood up from the park bench and put our hands in the air. The cops had us surrounded the whole time, but allowed a brief moment of freedom. More guns

● ● ●

than I cared to count were pointed at us; including a specialized tech team as insurance. All of our turrets were dismantled, our personal bugs disabled, and even my eye showed nothing but a blue screen. The arm became disabled now, and the cuffs latched onto our wrists.

Well mother, just another day in the Roman life eh? Maybe prison won't be so bad. I could use the shut-eye in all this. A light dusting of snow began to fall. I'm happy this is how the year ends, it's very romantic.

Anthony and I proceeded into the paddy wagon to go to our new home. Was this all a dream or a memory? Until I figure out the answer, all I can say is this:

Happy New Year…

Soundtrack List

SEVEN TRIBUTES TO THE BLUE BLOODS OF SILVER TREES AND SAINTS OF TAILORS

1. SNTS – Resurgence
2. Strapping Young Lad – Underneath the Waves
3. Grimes – My Sister Says the Saddest Things
4. Static-X – Machine
5. Edith Piaf – Non, je ne regrette rien
6. The Algorithm – Boot
7. Strapping Young Lad – Almost Again

Track Placement

1. Seraphim

2. Exhale

3. Naraka

4. Yin

5. Rand

6. Somatic

7. Nova

Closure

I hope you enjoyed this tale of sex, drugs, and rock'n'roll. To this day, I still don't quite remember how it came to be. As I stated earlier it was first started up in 2009, but my own insecurities and dying relationship got in the way. 10 years of dust collected…10 years lost…a reminder to myself to never let anyone get in the way of my dreams or else I'd simple wither away into a loser of nothingness.

To be honest though, all I want to do is shit, vomit, and cry and throw in the towel. In giving up the ideation of suicide, I have to play the long game and see what becomes of me in the future. Maybe my ex wishes a premature death on me, who knows? I wish her no harm; just miss the idea of starting a family together. Many projects…very little time…right now I just want a woman to calm me. Hugs, kisses…blowjobs. Dangerous creatures I realized, oh well!

With that said, I've just started the beginnings of my next project. It'll be my first true horror story: Miasma. "Never Being Me" is more of a psychological thriller compared to horror. This story will consists of more hallucinations, absolute terror, hidden secrets from history, and a subject I've been dying to touch on: Voodoo.

I also added a bonus picture in the back as a bit of fan service to those imagining that one scene with Tanya meeting Blue. And yes…I added the L.P.T gang again, and always will, because I love them to death. I enjoy being a silly mook!

Until we meet again…

Disclaimer

ISBN (Paperback) 978-1-7336856-2-7

Guy Maybriar Presents:

Lil Puddin Taters

Original concept: Guy Maybriar
Artwork: David Hernandez
Coloring: Guy Maybriar

L-R:
Virgil - Pug
Hubert - Song Sparrow
Floyd - Tabby Cat
Caleb - Little Penguin
Gunnar - Pacific Walrus

Their "Review" of Brother Roman

Virgil: "Worst.Hitman.Story.Ever! 1/5"
Hubert: "Decent until the end with Tanya...2/5"
Floyd: "The chicks were hot at least. 3/5"
Caleb: "And the drug dealer got his! 4/5"
Gunnar's Thoughts: (...Thinks stoically...5/5)

www.ingramcontent.com/pod-product-compliance
Lightning Source LLC
Chambersburg PA
CBHW050112280326
41933CB00010B/1072